TO ANNA

from

A. R. flum.

The natural healing force within each one of us is the greatest force in getting well.

—Hippocrates

Nature, time, and patience are the three great physicians.

—Chinese Proverb

We need to be brave, shaking off fear, particularly in times of change and transformation, and we need to have the courage to truly live our lives . . . . In the process of healing ourselves, we are better able to help to heal others. As the shamans have always known, the wounded healer heals.

—*Healing our Hearts and Lives,* Eileen Campbell

Chapter 1

So What's It All About?

The broad aim of this book is to help and inspire those on the road to recovery. The following account relates to the healing experiences of Andrew Penman, who in March 1989 was hit by a car and hospitalized. He then spent months in intensive-care and trauma departments of the University Hospital of Wales, Llandough Hospital in Cardiff, and Rookwood Hospital in South Wales. After the accident, his own determination to get well has led Andrew to spend more than a quarter of his lifetime healing himself with, of course, as he would readily recognize, the aid of others. Andrew's 'long unwinding road' has been a tortuous one. This book is an account of that journey, initia.lly based on extracts from his mother's diary and later on extracts from Andrew's own diary and a number of interviews of Andrew with the editor of this book.

Maybe you know someone who has suffered brain damage. This book may make a positive contribution towards that individual's healing. The book does not in any way claim to be medically objective or claim to offer a recommendation for treatment. It simply outlines the endeavours of one person in the sincere hope that others who might have suffered in a similar way to Andrew will derive inspiration from his post-accident experiences.

In a few words

The following account is a mix of Andrew's own words from extracts from diaries, which he has kept for nearly twenty-three years, together with interviews from 2006 and entries from his mother's diaries from the early days of Andrew's recovery, when he was unable to write. In the very early days, Andrew was also unable to speak or see.

Interviews

Information from e-mails sent and received between 2004 and 2005 have also been included in this account, bringing Andrew's remarkable story of healing up to date. The book also includes reports from newspapers, magazines, and other sources containing information from interviews the editor of this book conducted with Andrew at his home in Canton in Cardiff in January 2001.

In a nutshell

It is Andrew's desire that this publication will inspire others on the road to recovery. It has taken many years for Andrew to get himself well and truly back on his feet, and in his own words, he still has a ways to go. He feels sure, however, that he can help other sufferers to recognize that where there is a will, there is a way, and that many of the exercises and healing techniques that he has employed over the years can be used by others in their recovery.

The story is specifically for those who have suffered from brain damage as a result of a traumatic accident, but many on the road to recovery from other illnesses might draw real inspiration from it too.

Andrew kept a diary of his recovery, begun by his mother, for eleven years, and it is his intention that the extracts, showing what he has learnt, may reach more people than those he has managed to inspire through his actions and spoken words to date. These entries provide a first-hand account of what Andrew was trying to achieve step by step, day by day.

This book, he feels, is a strong starting point of a career in healing, which has been his long-term aim.

This book is only a small portion of the full story.

Background to Andrew's Story

Andrew Penman, born 20 February 1963, was struck by a car near the Canton Road Bridge in Cardiff in the early hours of the morning on Sunday, 6 March 1989. The damage to his body was considerable, but more seriously, he received a massive blow to the right side of his head. The doctors at the hospital in Cardiff concluded that he probably wouldn't survive the night, and even if he did, he would be massively handicapped and very unlikely to recover.

Andrew has recovered from that traumatic accident, which initially left him truly brain damaged. The long and unwinding road to recovery has been a road of determination and resolve, including his desire to use natural forms of healing in the form of dietary modifications, detoxification, short fasts, and martial arts.

After a night on the town, in which he now happily admits that he had been drinking far too much, Andrew was crossing the road and was hit head-on by a car, which then ploughed into a nearby bus shelter, taking him with it. To this day, Andrew has had no bad words for the driver, who tried to avoid hitting him. Andrew had attempted to run back to the pavement, only to be hit by the vehicle, which had swerved in order to avoid him. Looking back today, Andrew says that before the accident, his life was in tatters. He freely admits that he drank far too much and took just about any drugs offered to him.

He was a 'soft touch', he says, and 'easily led' to the demon drink.

His current lifestyle could not be more different than it was then. Before the accident, Andrew had lost himself in drink and had given up an active sporting life as a key player on the Cardiff CIACs youth rugby team.

Now an active member of the local community in Thailand, where he lives with his wife, Lalita, and in Wales when he returns, Andrew is involved in aikido, t'ai chi, and chi kung, three non-aggressive martial arts which have helped, along with a wide range of other healing techniques, both conventional and complementary, to help him get well again.

Andrew is determined to recover completely, and it is not difficult to imagine that this will be the case, having spent time talking to him about his healing experiences. I initially interviewed Andrew in Cardiff in 1998, after responding to an advertisement that he had placed in the local arts centre for an editor and writer to help him relate his account to a wider audience. This book is part of that attempt to reach people who might be inspired by his shift in lifestyle. Andrew is also going to produce an audio version of the book, and a Braille version is a real possibility. An audio version of his story containing recorded extracts and narrative will hopefully reach the ears of those people who have lost their sight as the result of an accident.

After his accident, Andrew was completely unconscious for four and a half weeks and seriously injured. He suffered massive bruising, broken ribs, and brain damage. After weeks of intensive care, he was left paralysed, unable to see, and unable to speak or recognize anyone.

As a youngster, Andrew loved sport, particularly rugby. He played centre, initially for Llandaff North youth rugby club and later for the infamous rugby outfit, in the South Wales region, at least, the Cardiff CIACS. In his working life, Andrew had been a builder and bricklayer, a strong young man who depended on his excellent co-ordination skills to help him at work and at play.

Prior to his accident, Andrew admits that his life was on the way down. He says, 'I was into drugs and booze in a big way . . . . I had a flat in Cathedral Road, in Canton' (a fairly select part of the city nowadays). 'I used to spend most of my time in city centre pubs drinking with my mates . . . . I really had no direction in life.'

Incredibly, he feels that the accident has actually done him a massive favour by giving him something to focus on, something to overcome.

He still likes his rugby, although he only watches these days. Of course, he never misses an international, but he prefers the comfort of his own flat either in Cardiff or in Thailand. The days of booze and drugs are long gone.

Unable to walk or speak at one point in his life, Andrew can now 'walk for miles', he says (unless he's fasting, part of a weekly

4

cycle of health treatments and exercises), and as I can testify, he can talk the hind leg off a donkey!

He puts his remarkable progress down to determination and a Buddhist spirituality backed up by his regular disciplines of aikido and t'ai chi, which he calls 'therapeutic for the brain as well as the body and [his] overall outlook on things'.

Andrew's mother's diary

Perhaps the best place to start his story is in March 1989, from the daily diary of his mum, who nursed him through the first few years after the accident.

The following extracts are his mum's own words.

> **Friday, 3 March.** Came back from Tenerife. Had a wonderful holiday.

> **Sunday, 5 March.** Traffic Police called 4 a.m. Andrew has had an accident at 3 a.m. Extensive head injuries, went to CRI [Cardiff Royal Infirmary Hospital], then to the Heath Hospital for scan, and then back to the intensive trauma unit. They haven't given much hope for him. We are all in a state of shock. Stayed at Hospital all night with Karen [brother's girlfriend at the time].

> **Tuesday, 7 March.** Stayed through the night with the twins. Slept for a few hours, [and] then went back. Heart and lungs have withstood the trauma; the first 36 hours are the worst they say.

> **Thursday, 9 March.** Stayed the night. Tonight [he] seemed very agitated and [was] coughing a lot, has chest infection. On ventilator, breathing some himself. I'm very worried. This seems to be a crisis point. This is the worst so far.

Monday, 13 March. [Andrew has now been moved to Llandough Hospital.] Andrew seems to be calmer here, probably the shock leaving his body. Has 'physio' a few times a day for his chest.

Tuesday, 14 March. Andrew stable. Julie [sister] went back to work today after being home a fortnight; she needs company and change of scene. Tracheotomy tonight.

Wednesday, 15 March. Andrew having great care and attention from the staff at Llandough Hospital.

Thursday, 17 March. We sit here for hours just talking to Andrew hoping he can hear us . . . .

21 March 1989. Dr. Davies [the neurologist] has told me that Andrew won't see or speak for a long time and he'll be a semi-invalid.

23 March. [I go to] hospital twice a day. Andrew still can't see or speak . . . . [He is] paralysed on the left-hand side.

25 March. Andrew's eyes are open, but still rolling.

29 March. [Andrew] moves his right leg . . . stares in front . . . head slumps forward.

31 March. [Still] no recognition of anyone. [H]ugely trying.

These days were clearly 'hugely trying' for the whole family, and as these statements show, it wasn't only Andrew who was traumatized. Doctors told him many months later that he wouldn't have survived the sheer shock of the impact of being hit by the car if he hadn't been so intoxicated.

These days he laughs at some of the terrible states he used to get into thanks to his consumption of drink and drugs. He remembers being very impressionable and easily led as a youngster.

Andrew has focused on an entirely different set of issues and priorities since the accident, perhaps mostly on the simple issue of living healthfully and enjoying the martial arts disciplines which have contributed so markedly to his recovery.

He feels an emerging ambition to be involved in healing in some way, and he feels that this book will inspire not only those who have suffered from head injuries, trauma, and shock but also those who have experienced any long-term medical condition and who feels they have a long road ahead.

> **11 May.** Saw doctor today. Doctor says that he has major head injuries . . . didn't give much hope of recovery.

> **16 May.** Every day much the same, slight improvement all the time.

> **21 May.** Threw his dinner at me in temper . . . head all mixed up.

At this point, there would have seemed to be little hope indeed, and those around Andrew probably thought that the doctors' prognosis was right. Andrew was in a real mess. He was uncommunicative, aggressive, and suffering from such considerable brain damage that physicians believed there could be little change in the future. Andrew has spent the time since proving them wrong.

Andrew out of hospital for the first time

3 June. Andrew home for the weekend . . . went to Sully with Karen.

5 June. Went down to the beach in his wheelchair . . . gets very tired.

11 June. Sleeping downstairs . . . still has no urine control . . . I have to change him in the night and his sheets.

19 June. He watches T.V. for a short while, but his eyesight is not too good . . . strength has not come back yet, he'll probably have glasses.

18 July. Andrew now recognizes friends and family . . . thinks he's [just] broken his legs and arm and will soon be up and about . . . but it is going to take a few years.

20 July. Saw Doctor today . . . . Andrew will be coming home for good in August . . . .

When the Physiotherapist at the infirmary said they would have him twice a week Andrew replied, 'No I want to come every day. So he had a taxi every day for intensive physiotherapy.

3 August. Everything ready for Andrew's homecoming, but he will be going back and fore to Rookwood for assessment. Also, he will be going to 'physio' at the Infirmary for six months.

4 August. Andrew came home today. Still in wheelchair, but can stand to go to toilet, but has to be helped to walk.

The kinds of problems that people who have suffered from brain injury might include the following:

Problems with understanding, memory, concentration, seeing, hearing, speaking, and thinking; moodiness; depression; antisocial or aggressive behaviour; difficulty expressing themselves; and changes in sexual drive. Andrew has at some time or other experienced all of these symptoms.

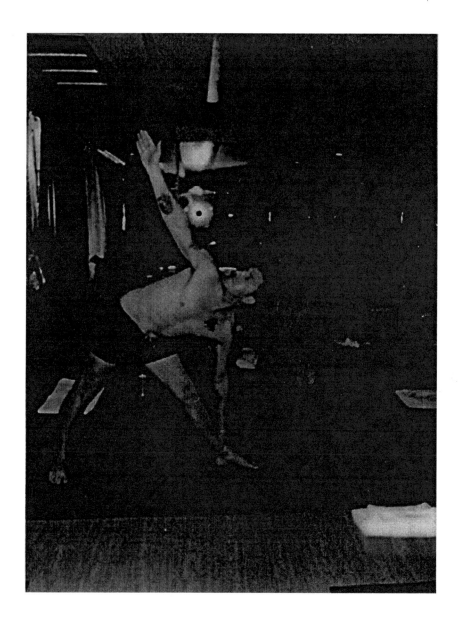

Extracts from Andrew's diaries will do the best job of communicating his side of the story. Additional commentary from articles published in the South Wales press have also been included in the pages that follow.

Andrew training in 2004 in Thailand.

Direct quotes from Andrew's mum's diary show the drama that the whole family went through. As always, it is not only the person who is ill who suffers but also those attending to that person. Those in attendance become part of the healing team and are drawn into and become responsible for the healing process. Andrew says that his *ongoing* recovery and development has been largely thanks to the benefits of martial arts and dietary changes, but in no small way, the help he has received from many people, family, friends, and professionals, has been important to him.

Andrew is highly motivated to tell other sufferers of brain injuries that he has hugely benefited from t'ai chi, aikido, and chi kung, all non-aggressive forms of martial arts that are gentle on the body and mind and help to restore coordination and clear thinking. The continuity and gentleness of many of the exercises has contributed greatly to Andrew's steady improvements. Of course, Andrew was not able to take part in martial arts until he had made significant improvements in his general strength, his perceptive abilities, and his overall body control. It took a lot of lonely walks, a lot of swimming, a lot of patience, and, of course, a lot of self-encouragement for him to reach a point at which he was able to contemplate taking part in martial arts. **Anyone contemplating using any of the exercises that Andrew mentions in this book, or indeed any of the exercises as seen in the pictures in this book, should first speak to a doctor, family members, and highly experienced martial arts professionals.**

Japanese insider in Hyaku
President Fukakusa

Andrew feels that the daily discipline of keeping a diary helped in his recovery. To introduce Andrew's mammoth diary, some extracts from his summary are presented.

These are the early days on the ladder of recovery. What was quite obvious was that Andrew was determined from the very start to succeed even though at times the road ahead was not so clear. He has said that when he was young, he would often wonder about how he would recover if he had an accident.

From being a boozer and drug taker and living off chips and other cheap and nasty fast food, Andrew has turned his passions for fitness and health-promoting disciplines into recovery. When some people are injured or end up in a wheelchair, they give up, accepting their fate. Not Andrew Penman. That was never going to be the way for him. Perhaps the following text from Andrew's summary sums up his attitude towards getting well via fitness, and his sense of humour, best.

Potty about timing myself

It's now midway through January '91. During the first year after the accident, I used to pee in a bottle. I first used to go in the room, or if anybody was there, mother would help me outside. I progressed back to the kitchen, which was about twenty yards away. I then walked to the corner of the street holding on to mother, around the three greens with Aunt Lorna, then to Brendan's, the newsagent's. It's all been a very slow job, but I never complained about doing the physio exercises. I was gradually walking farther and farther, and I spent most of early January that year doing walks or floor exercises if it was too wet. Of course, I wouldn't go out if it was windy, as I thought that I would get blown over!

I also bought a sit-up bench and had light dumbbells for fitness. I was admitted to Rookwood on 14 January 1991. I was potty about timing myself walking and exercising. I used to walk for hours until I came to a standstill with inflamed tendons. I used to mark my diary as though I were a schoolteacher or mad professor and give myself stars and make silly comments like 'very good', 'keep it up', 'not bad', etc. I used to go walking with and without the stick. On this one occasion I had two stars.

When I was in a wheelchair, I used to go to the toilet in a bottle. I would sit in the chair and hang on till the very last moment. It has a been a very slow job. The improvement was so slow that close family did not notice the improvements, but someone who sees me every couple of months does notice, and tells me, and this gives me great encouragement and makes me train all the harder.

It has all been a slow job, but as the well-worn motto goes: no pain, no gain.

The following extracts from Andrew's diary reflect the efforts he has put in over the years, the humour he has managed to sustain, and the natural-healing ideas that he has come across and put into practice.

Tuesday, 26 March. Swimming with Steven, sister's boyfriend. I have to be accompanied as I might lose my balance and slip.

I still do my exercises religiously, even if I have a full day elsewhere. Sometimes I'd get into bed knackered from a hard day's training, and if I had forgotten some exercise or other, I'd be up out of bed making sure that I didn't finish the day without it.

Tuesday, 16 April. Off to the skill centre for rehabilitation.

These were still the early days in Andrew's recovery. Andrew benefitted hugely from the attention of his relatives, especially his mum. Andrew would be the first person to say that he has been determined to get back on his feet, and as I can confirm, he's a positively stubborn person! He would also add, I'm sure, that teamwork has played a huge part in the recovery process. His team has included his wife in no small part over the last few years.

Asian Aikido International Festival, Bangkok, 2005

Wednesday. Debbie said people with my type of brain injury usually reach a plateau in their improvements, but Andrew trained himself through the plateau and kept on improving to this day and the rest of his long life. I've just realized that all the physical work that I have been doing has actually been helping the brain. This is why I am getting better.

Wednesday, 15 May. Physio Debbie says it's all up to me now. She's right.

Friday, 7 June. Time of release was dinner time. I was given a ball to play with to help my concentration.

Saturday, 8 June. I was told to walk with a stick to distribute weight evenly, as it was the left side that was paralysed.

11 June. No pain, no gain. No pain, no gain. No pain, no gain.

Debbie my physio said I'd be walking by Christmas!

Unaided

9 September 1991. Big achievement: went swimming in the Empire Pool[1] unaided for the first time. I was still on crutches though.

3 February 1992. Had a walk to town. Tuesday had a blackout, and I was taken to Cardiff Royal Infirmary Hospital and then on to Llandough Hospital, where I stayed overnight.

Lalita, Andrew's wife, at a training
session/symposium, Thailand, 2005
Photo: Yong Git

---

[1]   The Empire Pool was the old Olympic-sized (50 m) swimming pool at the site of present-day Millennium Stadium in Cardiff. It was built for the Commonwealth Games in Cardiff in the late 1950s.

Back in the early days

Monday, 10 January. Training with Bernard Chesney at Llanishen Centre. I carried on training in the house: press-ups, squat thrusts, and stretching. I also train at the sports centre. I like going there to meet people, to have a chat. At this stage I was going to the library for a walk and to get myself out of the flat. It was a terribly rainy day, so I rested, which I was glad of, as I'd done a lot the day before.

I was fasting, but not a proper fast, as I used to have a cup of water and fruit. I didn't start fasting till sometime in May. Knotted pains in my stomach. I used to go to Cogan to keep my mind off the pains.

Staying off dairy products. Fasting regularly and getting stronger and stronger.

In the next stage of Andrew's recovery, along with exercising, fasting, and dietary improvements, which included eating lots of fruit and vegetables, chicken, liver, and fish, was to get his mind into gear with French lessons, aikido, t'ai chi, word processing (which led to this book), and anything to help him regain his focus and concentration. 'You name it, I want it,' Andrew said. 'And, if it will help in my recovery, bring it on!'

8 February 1995. Empire Pool, did twenty lengths: front crawl, breaststroke, and backstroke. I could feel myself getting stronger and stronger. The health tablets I'm taking at the moment are selenium, lecithin, royal jelly, taurine, L. cystine, beta-carotene, glutamine.

Ready to live on my own again

16 February 1995. I am relying on Mother to do too many things for me, so I've started to make enquiries about a flat.

I'm now ready to live on my own again.

18 March 1995. This week I did aikido twice, swimming three times, and the gym three times.

Concentrating on aikido

Aikido has helped Andrew enormously with co-ordination, timing, and balance. This was an incredibly creative period for him. Through his training, he has developed confidence and strength. His diary reflects that this period was a real test. He had decided not to let his healing experience plateau but to battle on and take his recovery to greater heights all the time.

11 May. My diary has been a godsend.

4 September 1995. Today was a significant day on my road to recovery. I had phoned up Radnor Road with Lana, who praised me enormously about yoga and Severn Road about t'ai chi. Carried on with aikido Tuesdays and Thursdays, but I've been overdoing it again!

Christmas 1995. I've now been practicing detoxifying (in the form of light fasts) as a part of my healing program for one and a half years. I think I'm going to end up training people.

Monday, 5 February 1996. I've learned to rest when exhausted and to take it easy. Just went for a swim and worked on the computer. At the beginning of my physiotherapy treatment, I was told that there was only so much that the physio could do and the rest was up to me. This made me determined to learn to walk again.

Besides training my body, I knew that I had to train my mind, as I was suffering from short-term memory lapses, and my speech was impaired. I decide to take up evening lessons in French, word processing, and speech therapy.

In March 1995 I was introduced to Aikido, and I realized that this was what I had been looking for. I have been so inspired by the experience of Kanetsuka Sensei, who, through his own determination, got over cancer and fought his way back to health and fitness. Since practicing aikido, my memory, concentration, balance, and general fitness have all improved significantly. Sensei Peter Gillard asked me to write a letter for the aikido magazine. I did this, and it came out in March and was the start of great things to come.

Friday, 15 March 1996. Did the newsletter from aikido; done for me. I was feeling rather chuffed with myself. I haven't been to the gym since 24 February. I'm concentrating on aikido

President Fukakusa.
Andrew on the receiving end of instruction
in the finer arts!

Sunday, 31 March 1996. It was this day that I thought that I would like to publish a book.

About my accident and recovery: And here we are quite a few years later!

Monday. Just yoga. I gave aikido a miss. I did some stretching exercises in the house, which helps me to relax.

6 June 1996. Got the keys to the flat. A big step, but I think I can handle it!

Wednesday, 19 June 1996. Robert Taylor, my t'ai chi teacher, said that he was very pleased with my progress. Everything I do is geared towards helping my balance, co-ordination, and memory. I then went for my usual swim at the Empire Pool.

I did sixteen lengths. I later found out that this is half a mile.

The next day was aikido training up at Llanrumney Leisure Centre. Debbie, my physiotherapist, said that I have been overdoing it again on the walking, and I now have an inflamed ankle. Felt a lot better on Monday the 24th, and I resumed yoga and aikido classes.

By this stage, Andrew's diary regularly paid homage to the nurses, physiotherapists, doctors, and specialists who helped him this far. The whole process had been a very slow and drawn-out effort but one which clearly paid huge dividends.

Andrew is still improving, and many years after that accident, he still has a limp on his left side and gets about more slowly than he did before. This is a problem which he feels he can yet eradicate.

Andrew is an active member of the community in both Thailand and Wales and is learning Thai and Japanese as well as computer skills, including the use of the Internet. His long-term aim is to be involved in the healing arts, as he feels that he has learnt so much which he'd love to be able to pass on to others.

Roundup

In order to conclude something that has no conclusion, as it Is clear that the process of healing is ongoing, it might be best to refer to a few things that people have said about Andrew's development to present some unsolicited impressions of those who know Andrew Penman.

With his ever present and modest sense of humour, Andrew feels that these words, paraphrased from the famous pop band Chumbawamba, best describe his journey:

I get knocked down, but I get up again, 'cause they're never keep me down.

Darien Pritchard, massage teacher and Feldenkrais practitioner, Cardiff, February 2005

When I first met Andrew Penman six years ago, he walked quite awkwardly and was very stiff in the left side of his body as a result of a road traffic accident which had taken place nine years previously.

Over the next two and a half years, I used ideas and procedures from the Feldenkrais method of movement awareness in treatment sessions with him, focusing especially on helping him to become more supple and co-ordinated on his left-hand side. I did hands-on work on the treatment couch to promote suppleness in his trunk, and guided him through progressively more complex exercises focused on aspects of balance and co-ordination in standing, walking, bending, and twisting, which he then practiced on his own between sessions.

These homework exercises seemed to dovetail well with his martial arts practice, especially aikido, and I believe that they complemented each other. Due to his dedication to both of these practices, he progressed in a slow, consistent way. I have only seen him a few times in the last few years, but each time I have been impressed with how his body co-ordination has developed from when I first began working with him.

Peter Gillard, Fifth Dan Shidoin, chairman of the British Aikido Federation, 9 February 2005

When Andrew came to aikido, it was plain to see it was going to be a challenge for him, and indeed us! In truth we thought Andrew would only stick it out for a few weeks, but we didn't know Andrew! The path of Aikido is one of self-improvement through martial training, a way to overcome physical and mental attack without the use of force, to try to come into harmony with nature. As Andrew has written, he saw the example of our teacher here in the UK, Kanetsuka Sensei, who had overcome cancer. He made up his mind to try to follow Sensei's example.

Andrew is always searching for ways to help his mind and body. I am happy that aikido has been a pillar in that search. Over the years Andrew has persevered in his training, sometimes stubborn, sometimes frustrated, but always working hard to overcome the obstacles in his life. He also has become an example of perseverance and its rewards!

I know it is Andrew's wish to help others in similar situations. What can be better in this life than to give to others what help he can?

I wish him well in this task.

President Fukakusa, chief instructor of Rebukan Dojo and Chairman of the Aikido Association of Thailand

I have had the pleasure of teaching Andrew aikido for approximately two years or more since he entered our dojo in Bangkok. Everyone at the dojo has admired his spirit in continually coming to training and having a desire to learn and improve his techniques.

Aikido is a martial art that requires a practitioner to replicate as best as possible what the instructor demonstrates. This requires abilities in observation and physical replication of the required movements.

Andrew has improved remarkably within these twenty months and everyone is saddened to know that (temporarily, anyway) he is leaving Thailand and our dojo.[2]

Andrew has shown true spirit in his training from which many other students should take example.

Let's return to more extracts from Andrew's diary.

The bad old days and the good old days

Andrew has said that he always knew he'd have an accident and do everything he's doing at the moment to get back to health and fitness. Spooky!

> I remember vividly coming out of the coma. I thought I was in a prison and that all the nurses were prison guards. I remember the curtains being pulled around me, then I was dressed, bundled into a wheelchair, and pushed to the table for breakfast.

---

[2]   Andrew left the dojo and Thailand temporarily to return to Britain to promote his book.

I was in a coma for four and a half weeks. I left hospital in a wheelchair and was on sticks and crutches for years before I finally decided that I didn't need them anymore.

First of all, I would walk around the house holding on to the walls and anything that I could lay my hands on, then I would go for short walks. At first I could only manage to walk across the road, rest for a while, and then hobble back.

The next stage was swimming, which has turned out to be one of the best things that I have done. I would get great encouragement from people telling me how much I had improved.

I would get into the changing room, leave my crutches on top of the locker, and hobble very slowly, holding on to the walls. I would get into the water and go straight into freestyle stroke. When I had completed a length, I would stop and tread water for a while before starting off again.

This book is not the place to publish the whole of Andrew's diaries, but a fuller version will be published at some point in the future once Andrew has attracted the interest of a bigger publisher, enabling many to read and share in many of the special moments in his long struggle against very nasty odds.

> At this stage I could not go out on my own and was still in my wheelchair, using a walking stick for very short distances. I was putting on weight, which was to be expected, as I wasn't getting about much. I was smoking, and I had to be watched constantly just in case I set fire to the house.
>
> I had a day's physiotherapy at Rookwood Hospital on 4 October 1989. It was decided that I needed to come to occupational therapy as well as physiotherapy every day.
>
> The Christmas party was at Rookward, and Linda took me and mother. The nurses were very pleased to see me.
>
> Up to 1990, I continued with the therapy and my own exercises with light dumbbells, sit-ups, and general fitness.
>
> My mother wanted me to go to a faith healer, so went along open-minded. The faith healer and the reflexologist were husband and wife (Nigel and Pat). He sat me down on a chair in the room, stuck his hands on my knee, and went into a sort of trance. I felt a pulling sensation, then he put his hands on my head, and I felt all the heat from his hands.
>
> I was feeling more confident about the future. We continued going for about six months. People

usually only go a few times, but as long as it was doing me some good, we kept going.

2 January 1991. The beginning of the year started as well as can be expected under the circumstances. I had bought a bench for sit-ups and general fitness. I was going out for walks, timing myself. Things plodded along, and I could see myself improving all the time.

Monday, 21 January. Physio twice a day. Walked inside hospital without a stick, too cold to go out. Much the same Tuesday, Wednesday, Thursday.

Saturday, 2 February 1991. I exercised for fifty-five minutes after a short walk.[3]

Sunday, 10 February. Arm exercises five minutes, general exercises for fifty-five minutes, went for a walk with mother, ten minutes on the fitness bike, opened bowels. Gave myself one star and commented 'not bad' considering the weather.

Friday, 15 February. Feeling generally okay. Dr McCoy has just diagnosed me as having acute gamblingitis caused by trying to beat the boredom of everyday life.

Sunday, 24 February. Rainy and blustery. Exercises twenty minutes and fifteen-minute arm exercises. Went walking for one hour. Walked without stick to Seven Oaks Park. For this effort, I gave myself two stars, ticked it, and commented, 'very good, keep it up'.

---

[3] When Andrew uses the term *walking*, he means moving with pronounced difficulty on both legs.

1 March (St David's Day). Walked down to the bookie's the long way around (fifty minutes), down the shops with my mother (thirty-five minutes) without stick!

2 March. I was thinking, 'There must be more to life than this,' but I was enjoying what I was doing and I knew that I wouldn't *always* be like this.

Wednesday, 13 March 1991. Went walking in the morning with and without stick. Arm exercises five minutes, stretching five minutes, sit-ups fifteen minutes, opened bowels, bath at the end of the day.

Friday, 15 March. I've cut down my walking to two and a half hours a day, as my heel is starting to give way as a result of doing too much.

Monday, 18 March. Gave up smoking.

Asian Aikido International Festival, Bangkok, 2005

Andrew on the receiving end of instruction in
the finer arts!

It was Andrew's decision to learn to drive. He started off in a manual car but had no coordination with the foot pedals, so he changed to an automatic. He started instruction in 1998 with the BSM Driving School and had many instructors. He then met Bob, a driving instructor for people with disabilities. He still had instruction from other instructors but always came back to Bob. On 6 January 2012, he passed his driving test in an automatic.

His decisions to get involved in t'ai chi, aikido, and in chi kung in order to help his balance, concentration, and general willpower and his decision to learn the skill of detoxification through fasting and to continue with swimming, free-weights exercises, and visits to the gym all showed his determination to get well.

His initial efforts concentrated on walking well, getting his strength and balance back, and slowly but very surely learning to speak once again.

Andrew is still improving, and many years after that accident, he still has a limp on his left side, a problem which he feels he can yet eradicate.

Life was getting better all the time, although there were times when my speech was letting me down badly and I felt awkward in certain social situations. I had been concentrating on the physical side of my recovery so much that I was forgetting to socialize as you might. Drinking was of course out of the question, but the local arts centre became a place that I'd go to from time to time. Then towards Christmas 2002, I came across an advert for a company that introduced British men to Thai ladies, and with the view of finding a compatible and caring partner, I got in touch with them. As I hadn't had much luck with local lasses for a while, I decided to get myself down to that sunny country and, well, as they say, the rest is more or less history. I now split my time between two countries that I love, Wales and Thailand. My current fitness program consists of aikido sessions twice a week, swimming three or four times a week, with Bikram yoga on most days.

My wife, Lalita, deserves more than a special mention, of course, as she's the one that keeps me going and who teaches me Thai with the patience of a Bangkok monk!

Photos: Lalita Penman

In the midst of winter, I finally learned that there was in me an invincible summer.

—Albert Camus

He who can believe himself well will be well.

—Ovid

The pessimist sees the difficulty in every opportunity; the optimist the opportunity in every difficulty.

—L. P. Jacks

Special Thanks:

To my mother, who gave up her life to look after me; the twins, Linda and Lorna, who helped me on my long walks; Peter Gillard, who has helped me to get where I am in aikido; and to Kanetsuka, who has overcome cancer and been a great inspiration to me. And of course to my lovely wife, Lalita, who continues to support me in everything I do. She has the patience of a priest. She's considerate and caring and great fun to be with.

Also, special thanks to Rob the computer boffin who helped me with my word processing, and Debbie, my first physiotherapist, who gave me encouragement at a crucial stage. She got me on my feet and said that the rest would be up to me.

In the early days she said that I would be up on my feet by Christmas (the first Christmas, that is), and I took it to mean that I would be walking around, but, in fact, she meant just standing up! I suppose my optimism was a way of keeping myself in the dark about the reality of the situation.

There have been countless others who have spurred me on, but my final thanks go to Sister Lloyd at Rookwood Hospital, who kept me in order.

Thailand Yoga

Andrew, second from the right. This photo was
taken fifteen years after the accident and getting
back to fitness, 28 October 2005.
Sensei Peter Gillard, Arcot Street, Penarth

Commitment, Self-help, and Healing

I was told I would become a healer by Brian Snelgrove up at
the students' union So I tried many things: shiatsu (foundation
and intermediate), chi kung healing, and reiki. Now I think aikido
and t'ai chi are the ones.

Driver and Vehicle
Licensing Agency
Asiantaeth Trwyddedu
Gyrwyr a Cherbydau

Keep this safe/Cadwch hwn yn ddiogel   7178581

Counterpart Driving Licence/Gwrthddalen y Drwydded   D740W

Important document – The photocard and paper counterpart should be kept together. Both must be produced when required.
Dogfen bwysig – Fe ddylai'r cerdyn llun a'r gwrthddalen eu cadw gyda'u gilydd. Rhaid dangos y ddwy pan fydd angen.

ANDREW RAYMOND PENMAN
31 WARWICK STREET
CARDIFF
CF11 6PW

85000

Document number/Rhif dogfen
120182520202

Driver number/Rhif gyrrwr
PENMA 602203 AR9RV

Issue number
Rhif cyhoeddi
86A

A.R.Penm.

I wybod mwy am wasanaethau Trwyddedau Gyrru ar-lein ewch i
www.direct.gov.uk/driverslicence
Find out more about Driving Licence online services at
www.direct.gov.uk/driverslicence

Provisional Entitlement
Hawl dros dro

Entitlement history (see Section 3 overleaf)
Cyn Hawllau Gyrru (Gweler Adran 3 dros y dudalen)

Category Categori	From O	Until Tan	Codes Codau	Category Categori	From O	Until Tan	Codes Codau	Category Categori	From O	Codes Codau
A	12 07 86	19 02 33								
B	01 04 80	19 02 33								
BE	19 01 12	19 02 33								
GH	01 04 80	19 02 33								

Endorsements (as supplied by Convicting Court)
Ardystiadau (fel y'u cyflwynwyd gan y Llys a'ch cafodd yn euog)

Convicting Court code Cod y Llys euogfarnu	Date of conviction Dyddiad yr euogfarn			Offence Code Côd y trosedd	Date of offence Dyddiad y trosedd			Fine Dirwy £	Disqual. period Cyfnod gwaharddi	Other Arall	Penalty points Pwyntiau cosb
	Day Diwrnod	Month Mis	Year Blwyddyn		Day Diwrnod	Month Mis	Year Blwyddyn				

NOTE: < means "earlier than"
SYLWER: < yn golygu "cyn"

You may only drive the above if you hold current
entitlement for a higher category

Cewch yrych uchod dim ond os oes gennych chi hawl
gyfredol ar gyfer categori uwch

Official Use
At Ddefnydd y Swyddfa

Changes to your permanent address, please write clearly in the boxes using CAPITAL LETTERS IN BLACK INK. (See Section 5 overleaf)
Newidiadau i'ch cyfeiriad parhaol, ysgrifennwch yn glir yn y blychau gan ddefnyddio LLYTHRENNAU BRAS MEWN INC DU. (gweler Adran 5 dros y dudalen)

New house No.
Rhif ty newydd

New Post Code
Côd Post newydd

New address
Cyfeiriad newydd

This document must not be used for change of name. For change of name please fill in and send us a 'Application for a driving licence' (D1) form, which is available to order from www.direct.gov.uk/motoringforms and to pick up at Post Office® branches / Ni ddylech ddefnyddio'r ddogfen hon os yw eich enw wedi newid. Os yw eich enw wedi newid, anfonwch ffurflen 'Cais am drwydded yrru cerdyn llun' (D1W) i ni, sydd ar gael i archebu wrth www.direct.gov.uk/motoringforms ac ar gael o ganghennau o Swyddfa Bost®.
Send the filled in form with your photocard and counterpart licence to DVLA, Swansea, SA99 1BN.
Llenwch y ffurflen a'i hanfon gyda'ch trwydded cerdyn llun a gwrthddalen y drwydded i DVLA Abertawe SA99 1BN.

Asiantaeth
weithredol o'r
Adran Drafnidiaeth
An executive agency of the
Department for
Transport

Sign in the white box
to confirm changes
Llofnodwch yn y blwch gwyn
i gadarnhau'r newidiadau

A.R.Penm.

Date
Dyddiad

7178581   60059 / 1005887044 / 0045

DSA
DRIVING STANDARDS AGENCY
SAFE DRIVING FOR LIFE

T 686305 5

Issue No.	Fee	Rem Type	O/D	S/C	T/P

PRACTICAL DRIVING
TEST PASS CERTIFICATE

This is to certify that:

Name _Andrew Pearson_

Driver Number $\boxed{P|E|N|M|A|6|0|2|2|0|3|A|8|9|A|\checkmark}$

Has Passed

| Category | | B | automatic yes / ~~no~~ | extended ~~yes~~ / no |

restriction code $\boxed{40.78}$

On _6/1/11_ At _Cardiff West_

Signature of Driving Examiner

Name of Driving Examiner _Tony Bloo_

Applicant's Declaration (only to be completed if sending this certificate to the DVLA)

I apply for a full driving licence for the category shown on this form and declare that there has been no change in my health since I last applied for a driving licence.

Applicant's Signature: Date / /

INVESTORS IN PEOPLE

IMPORTANT
PLEASE READ THE NOTES OVERLEAF

T 686305 5

DSA 10
Rev (03/11)

Albany Language School

45, Monthermer Road , Cathays, Cardiff U.K. CF24 4QX ~ 02920 215565

Certificate

In the

Teaching of English as a Foreign Language

(One to one and small class groups)

~ This is to certify that the candidate ~

.... Andrew Penman................

Has achieved a pass or higher in each of the assignments presented ~~~~~ ~~~~~

and has been awarded a grade

B

~ Signature ~

....

~ date ~

April 25th 2005

Director : Roger Knight Bsc. F.E.T.C. Cert TEFL Cert Lit
D32 D33 (tdlb)

Consultant Tutor   :   Osma Nasir M.A. TEFL

Albany Language Services   ~
regd with The NATIONAL LANGUAGES FORUM
With recognition and support from ELWA, Wales' leading training agency.
Teaching practice in Thailand.

Albany Language School is an International School of English based in Cardiff,
Europe's youngest Capital.

WHAT AIKIDO HAS DONE FOR ME

by Andrew Penman

In March of 1989 I was involved in a road traffic accident and sustained serious head injuries with swelling on the brain. My chances of survival were slim. I was to spend five months in hospital. In the Intensive Care Infirmary at Llandough I was given an emergency tracheotomy and was in a coma for four weeks on a ventilator. My memory and speech were non-existent and I was paralysed down my left side. Later I was transferred to the Rockwood Hospital in Llandaff for rehabilitation and extensive radiotherapy. In August I was discharged from hospital; but went to the Cardiff Royal Infirmary daily in a wheelchair for speech therapy and physiotherapy.

All this had been organised for me, of course; but in 1991 I decided to start doing things for myself. I started very slowly with crutches, taking short walks, each day going a bit further. The doctors at the hospital were very pleased with my progress, since - as is often the case - I did not reach a plateau; and I progressed to using two sticks for six months, then one stick, and finally in 1993 no sticks.

At the very beginning of my physiotherapy treatment I was told that there was only so much my instructors could do: the rest was up to me. This made me determined to succeed in learning to walk. I tried many sports but at the beginning I found training with other people too hard, so I tried a different though exacting approach. For two years I trained with light weights, then changed to sit-ups, slow press-ups, squat thrusts, pull-ups, finishing with a rowing machine and a bike to have a good sweat.

All this gave me a firm body and a degree of fitness, but I still hadn't really found what I needed. Besides training my body I knew I had to train my mind, as I was suffering from short term memory lapses and my speech was impaired. I decided to take some evening courses, which included French

lessons, word processing and speech therapy. Not only did this help my concentration; I learnt to converse with people and regained some self-confidence. But I still wasn't satisfied.

In March 1995 I was introduced to Aikido and I realised that this was what I had been looking for. I have been very much inspired by the experience of Kanetsuka Sensei, who through his determination overcame his cancer and fought his way back to health and fitness. Since practising Aikido my memory, concentration, balance and general fitness have all improved significantly; and this improvement has been noticed not only by me but by others too. I have also tried Tai Chi and found that the movements helped my concentration and balance; but I've found Aikido much more beneficial to my needs.

To keep myself occupied I do some training every day. Since joining the Aikido group in Cardiff I find myself more confident in going to practices at night - something I have not felt with other kinds of training. I feel I'm improving all the time, and in August 1995 I went to the B.A.F. Summer School in Chester. I had a great time and I'll certainly be going again.

I've come a long way from exercising alone in the house with dumbells and squeezing soft balls; walking up and down the stairs, walking sideways, crossing one leg over the other, in the hall! I have been very lucky: everything I've done in my recovery has come at the right time, and discovering Aikido seems of all things to have helped me most. The exercise helps my body (even though sometimes I don't feel up to it, Im always glad afterwards). Its like advanced physiotherapy. My balance, concentration and memory have all benefited; and it has boosted my confidence a great deal. I look forward to continuing my practice for many years to come.

(Andrew Penman is a member of the Sho Bu Kan Dojo, Cardiff)

武道 THE IDEALS OF JAPANESE BUDO

(Extract from the Hombu Dojo Aikido Training text)

Japanese Budo (Martial Ways), although developed from techniques of bloodshed (bujutsu), have taken as their main purpose and ideal the qualities of harmony and love, or the path to self-realisation. This is the essence of Japanese Budo and it is especially apparent in Aikido, which includes techniques from the traditions of ju-jutsu, where one faces an adversary empty handed.

One old precept of the martial arts of ancient Japan is called Shin-bu fu-satsu, meaning literally 'divine bu, no killing'. It means that the way of killing or causing injury to another is a cause of shame. Many of the bujutsu (martial arts) rather than emphasising the aim of getting a head-start in battle by attacking first, trained the warrior to learn to adjust his movements in accordance to those of the enemy and then to find ways of attacking his weak points. To achieve this, to be able to have the enemy's life in the palm of your hand, requires that you build up a massive store of shugo (austere training) and sufficient confidence.

Sports, on the other hand, use artificially constructed rules which are designed to give victory to the person who excels in relative terms of more speed, more strength or more size.

The ideals of budo are not to be simply inscribed on some tablet inside your own head; rather they are to be concretely and solidly grasped, through relationships with other people, by making your entire spirit, mind and body your target.

nocn
NATIONAL OPEN
COLLEGE NETWORK

Hyn sydd i dystio bod / This is to certify that

Andrew Penman

wedi cyflawni / has been awarded

6 Credyd ar Lefel Dau / Credits at Level Two

ar raglen o'r enw / on a programme entitled

Sport and Exercise Sciences

a ddarparwyd gan / provided by

Coleg Powys

Unedau a gyflawnwyd / Units achieved

Teitl yr Uned Unit Title	Côd Unit Code	Credyd(au) Credit(s)	Lefel Level
Modiwl/Module: Rugby Attacking Set Plays - Rugby	MG3/2/CY/007	3	Dau / Two
Defending set piece plays	MG3/2/CY/009	3	Dau / Two

rhca
CYMRU

ocn
WALES

Janet Barlow

Janet Barlow
Prif Weithredwr / Chief Executive Officer
Rhwydwaith Coleg Agored Cymru
Open College Network Wales

Jill Brunt
Prif Weithredwr / Chief Executive
Rhwydwaith Coleg Agored Cenedlaethol
National Open College Network

Rhif Cofrestru/Registration No: 73229
Dyddiad Dyfarnu/Award Date: 18/07/2008
Rhif Tystysgrif/Certificate No: 3343650

CQFW

Local news

£25,000 blitz on litter is starting

A £25,000 litter blitz has begun on Cardiff's river-banks.

The move is the latest phase in a Wales-wide clean-up project by Keep Wales Tidy.

Teams of volunteers and contractors will tackle the trees and foliage, which traps litter, alongside the Rivers Taff and Ely.

Cardiff County Council's waste management department and Cardiff Harbour Authority have backed the city's campaign.

Keep Wales Tidy hopes that once the cleanup has begun, community groups and local businesses will "adopt" stretches of riverbank to keep litter-free.

This would assist the work of two local volunteer groups who already work to keep litter at bay in Ely and Llanrumney.

Work has already

Survivor Andrew

LIVING TO TELL THE TALE Andrew Penman has made an amazing recovery, having to learn to walk and talk again, after being hit by a car in Canton in March 1989.
PICTURE: Andrew Davies

In Brief

History will come to life

THE history and heritage of Wales is set to come to life this weekend at a popular tourist attraction.

Attractions at Llancaiach Fawr Manor, in Nelson, will include dance and music performances, dramatic presentations and talks on traditional foods.

There will also be flag-making, poetry and painting workshops for children.

For more details, call 01443 412248.

Table-top sale

A TABLE-top sale is being held tomorrow at Christchurch, on the corner of Waterhall Road and Pwllmelin Road, in Fairwater, Cardiff.

Open from 10.30am to 1pm, tables cost £5 and can be booked by calling 029 2055 3507.

Class on move

A SLIMMING World class, which is currently held at the United Reformed Church, Windsor Place, Cardiff, is moving to a new venue.

The class, from 11.30am to 1.30pm, will now be held every Monday at the Cardiff Ex-Servicemen's Club, at Charles Street, Cardiff.

Next dance date

SOUTH Wales Rock'n'Roll Club's next dance will be held on Friday, March 23 at the

ref- Andrew Jephcun. 01074-610686.

LAST 2 Years I've lived up Brecon. I'M ~~married~~ MARRIED

and doing a DIPLOMA in sports and science up

Brecon college and have completed 1st year of

a 2 Year curse.

there are a lot of useful things on

Discs, which roger kept and not use in

script.

My websites are (1) http://web.ukonline.co.uk/ar. penma *expired!*

(2) ~~███████████~~

and I swim and train in Atheralo up

Brecon beac.

and I have my ~~Driving~~ Test on 1st September

in Automatic Car.

the web Sites have not been up dated

for a couple of years.

I was awarded 2ª KYU in thailand for karate

A.R. Penman.

where I lived for 2 was Going have every 6 mth.

sports council wales
cyngor chwaraeon cymru

Great Coaches...Great Sport

sports coach UK

is pleased to confirm that

Andrew Penman

has attended

on

25th February 2008

Patrick Duffy
Chief Executive

sports coach UK
certificate of attendance

Andrew Penman

8 November 2011

To whom it may concern,

I have known Andrew for over ten years as his aikido instructor. I believe Andrew is a hard worker, and when he is set on a task will try his best to see it through.

I know personally that over the years since his accident, Andrew has never given up or asked for help but has held a strong belief in himself to improve every day!

I hope Andrew would be given every chance to show his capabilities, and I am sure that given that chance, he will give 100 per cent.

Yours faithfully,

Peter Gillard

Chapter 2

I had an accident in March 1989. I was in a coma for four and a half weeks. I was in hospital for five months, which was a bit of a miracle considering the injuries I sustained. I sustained an injury to the right side of the brain, which left me paralysed on the left side. I couldn't see or speak and was nearly a cabbage. Visitors used to bring salt and pepper to sprinkle on the cabbage. (Just joking.) A clinical psychologist I saw said people with my types of injuries usually experience a mildly euphoric state, which means they're happy all the time. But I was like that before the accident, always joking around. But when I got on to the demon drink, I just went crazy-aid *bonkers*. Then I started to smoke ganja, and it soon led me to take more potent things, such as magic mushrooms, acid, and speed, but it didn't stop there. I didn't start smoking cigarettes till I was seventeen. I got in with the wrong crowd, but it was mainly my fault; I was easily led. I always knew I'd have an accident and be doing everything I'm doing at this time. Everything is happening now just as I used to think it would and as I envisioned when fishing for eels over at the Taff and at ponds and doing other activities. I left hospital in a wheelchair and was on crutches for years. Gradually I got stronger and stronger through my own determination. I always knew I'd be doing everything I possibly could to get back to health and fitness. I was in hospital from March to August. I was determined to walk, so I exercised religiously three times a day. They had me in Rookie [Rookward Hospital] for physiotherapy, as they could see the improvement I was making.

I didn't realize how serious my injuries were. When the physiotherapists said I'd be walking by Christmas, I thought that I would be hopping and skipping, just like you see in the films. So I continued to do my exercises so I could walk before Christmas. I suppose it was the brain keeping me in the dark about how serious my injuries really were.

I was lucky in many ways that everything I did came at the right time for my improvement, such as Channel View, where I used to lift light weights fast, to get a good sweat on, and Empire

Pool. Both are now closed down, but they did me good. They used to get me out mixing with people. My brain was still improving. My speech was very quiet, but my therapists discharged from speech therapy saying there was nothing wrong with my speech; it was just very quiet due to the tracheotomy. The doctors gave me this when I was in a coma and had a chest infection to help me breathe. Back to Empire Pool and Channel View: I used to hobble up to Empire Pool on my crutches, leave them on top of a locker, and make my way very slowly, holding on to walls, into the water. I started off very slowly, doing half widths, and gradually built my stamina up to lengths. I had a lot of help from the lifeguards; one who was particularly good was Barry. I also used to go to an improvers' course run by Jean on a Monday and a free lesson taught by students on a Friday. I got very fit. Well, as fit as you could expect for someone with my predicament. I used to joke around saying I was the fittest cripple in Great Britain. At that stage, I would joke around saying ridiculous things. I would go to Channel View by taxi and do my training for one hour. Then eventually I would go swimming straight away. Up at the hospital they told me not to do this, but I was one of the first brain-injured persons they had treated, so I learned by my mistakes, sometimes ending up worse off but most of the time coming through unscathed.

I met an old school friend (Paul Bowing) down at the sports centre. He used to pick me up and give me a lift. He worked on the door over a club down at the docks with Bernard Chezney, who was the trainer the Llanishen circuit squad and for Great Britain's Paralympics team, and Bowing told Chezney about me. So we arranged a training session, and I used to train twice a week with him.

We used to do sit-ups, press-ups, squat thrusts, and burpees. I used to regard myself as one of them at this stage, but I couldn't be with them, as they would bring me down to their level. I was taken to Highfields in the beginning after the accident, but it was for people who are born with disabilities and don't know any different.

I haven't yet looked at my diaries: I'm doing all this from memory. I'll inform you when I am.

I would walk for miles in the early stages, even with sprained ligaments in my ankle. When my bounce was okay, as far as I was concerned anyway, I used to catch the bus from the station (on my crutches) and hobble to Severn Road School, where I started French lessons to get out and mix with people. I had a good spirit and was being guided. At Severn Road I also joined a math, an English, and a computer course, which helped my brain enormously. I was drawn to t'ai chi at Severn Road. I saw people doing strange movements with their hands and feet. I was very interested in these people doing strange movements and joined them. I always knew I'd have an accident and be drawn into the Eastern way of life. They are years ahead of us as far as the mind is concerned. We're just understanding things that they've known in the East for generations.

I was going over to a neighbour's house. She was a staff nurse up at Rookie and a Jehovah's Witness. After a while she roped me into going to a meeting with her in Canton. I went along for somewhere to go and ended up going regularly for two years. It was excellent therapy for me. I got me out socialising and meeting people and, last but not least, allowed me to air my suit. I used to go training at secluded gyms with other Jehovah's Witnesses, and we arranged a holiday to Ibiza in Spain for two weeks. We had a flight over and settled in. I soon found out what the Jehovah's Witnesses were all about. The one I used to go weight training with was like me: he was just going for something to do and somewhere to go, but the other fellow was hooked on it. Jehovah had brainwashed him. I fell out with them, as they wouldn't go out to socialize. They were like kids on a school trip, buying cans of beer from the supermarket and staying in to drink them. At this stage I could walk for miles, and I found a pub on the outskirts of town managed by a Welshman. I used to go on long walks there. A flight was available to come home, so I took it. It was an experience coming all the way from Spain, flying then catching the train. The Jehovah's Witnesses would slowly brainwash you without your knowing it. I've seen many ex-Jovies. But it was part of my recovery. It taught me to socialize, meet all different races, and, of course, I used to air my suit once a week.

I started my aikido training on 14 March 1995. I've improved leaps and bounds since then. I was walking very slowly, as had no balance, but the aikido has been really good. I treat my sessions as physiotherapy. It is now midway through January 1999, so it's nearly ten years since the accident. I'm going to Japan to practice aikido, which will be a big achievement. I've come on tremendously well, considering my injuries, and now I think that there's nothing really wrong with me. Aikido is a lifelong martial art. You will still learn to your dying day.

I was down at the sports centre training with light weights when I met Roy Court. We got talking, and he arranged for me to do judo down at the Howardian Centre. I continued going there for a short period, but that didn't last, as I didn't really mix with the disabled. It was an experience throwing people around.

I was to have my last visit to Rookie 11 April 1995. The last couple of days before I was to be discharged, I was fed up with patients being depressed and feeling sorry for themselves whilst I was walking about as if nothing had really happened. I'd just had a bad accident. It was my brain that had swelling and bruising, but luckily it all settled down. I was lucky that I had no bad breaks, just fractures.

I had a driving assessment on 13 July. I had several lessons with hand controls for gears (an automatic transmission). I had a driving lesson in December, but the driving instructor was just taking my money off me. We'd be driving along and I would veer to my left. This went on for a while, and each time he would pull me over to straighten us up.

On 26 October 1995, I came home from aikido by bus with sweat pouring off me. I had caught a virus but still managed a session, but then I was off for a week.

On 20 November 1995 I tried the David Lloyd centre. They had a few massive gyms, but all the people there were snobs and yuppies, so I gave that place a miss. Fees were far too dear and the location was right out of the way. It would have meant taking taxis, and at this stage I was watching my money.

On 28 November 1995 I bought a computer and word processor. I met a man in t'ai chi who showed me what to buy and how to use it. He still comes around my flat to help me occasionally, and I phone him up quite often. He started me off on my new word processor, as the other one packed it in. I bought a brand-new portable typewriter that also prints also. It's intended mainly for office work, so it's not really on the market yet. I was lucky to hear of a place that sold them and thought that would be ideal for me. At this stage I'd still be going to Llanishen Leisure Centre the sports centre to do my light weights and aerobic work as well as going to aikido twice a week and swimming three times a week. I also went on long walks of up to an hour three times daily for therapy and to get out of the house. At this stage I couldn't keep still for very long. I had to be doing something or going somewhere all the time. But I realized that actual rest is just as important as training. Christmas went well considering the predicament I was in.

January 1996. On 2 January I had a walk up to the Friary to see about word processing and computing classes. I continued to go swimming in the Empire Pool and practice aikido. I had pulled my shoulder in aikido and was taking it easy, just going for a gentle swim, as it is a healer for my body. I was going to give myself a complete rest, but saying that, I'd still be doing exercises in the house.

I started yoga in Radnor Road from 7.30 to 9.00 and continued to go swimming in the afternoon for my routine on a Monday. Tuesday I would go to aikido, Wednesday I would go to t'ai chi from 1.00 to 3.00 and then for a swim up at Empire Pool. Thursday was aikido. I paid for a course in the Friary for ten weeks, but I only went a few times. I would be still going to the sports centre's gym as well as to aikido in the evening. I was still learning about the body all the time. I was really going to keep busy and fill the days up at this stage.

At the end of January, the 26th to be precise, I gave up driving lessons as the instructor had to keep pulling the wheel as I would veer to one side due to brain injury. I'm working up slowly to being able to manage my own computer. On 3 February I went on an aikido course with Kanetsuka Sensei from 5.00 to 7.00. I also went for a swim in the morning and on Sunday from 1.00 to 3.00. At this stage I was relying on my mother too much and time was flying, but also I was not getting any younger. I decided I'd like to live on my own for my own independence and because I had very weird ways. They told me at the hospital about the weird things that brain-injured people get up to, but I never thought that would apply to me. I viewed a few flats, and then one came up in Canton which was perfect for me: a nice self-contained flat, so I purchased it out of my settlement. I was in aikido's newsletter for March about the accident and doing aikido. I hadn't been to the gym since 24 February. I was concentrating on aikido, courses at schools, and swimming, which was very important. I was learning to relax. I relaxed with a record player and CD system I bought.

I did my work on the word processor and shopped for fruit and veg. I blended my veg and ate it raw. I was learning about the brain all the time and have learned to relax completely in aikido. But it's easier said than done. Of course, aikido is the most difficult martial art to learn. It's a very, very slow job, but there's no rush, as you've got the rest of your life to go. It's an experience. You don't become a black belt in a couple of years like in other martial arts. Aikido is all about your chi energy work. I had a shiatsu class in Severn Road. I was drawn to this by the spirits: I went on the course for a namesake, Tony Penman. There aren't many people of the name Penman about. But I class myself as a Jones (my mother's name). The course went really well. I didn't really know what shiatsu was, but it was an excellent stretch for the back. Next day was Sunday, and I fasted. I'd been doing this for one year and nine months. On the Monday I had booked a shiatsu appointment at a practitioner's private clinic in Cathedral Road. It went really well. The practitioner worked on my lower back and hips, and he commented that I had a strong spirit. I booked another appointment. I rested for the next couple of days from aikido and swimming and my gym work, although I carried on with my long walks up town. Shiatsu took it out of me. By Thursday I was fine for aikido in the evening from about 8.30 to 10.00. Next day I was knackered after aikido and went for my usual long walk up town and then for a swim on the way home to my mother's. I swam eleven lengths and treaded water. No pain, no gain, as I used to state. I then had a restful weekend watching sports.

At this stage I practiced my typing skills, getting used to the keyboards on word processors, and I decided that I was going to write a book about the accident from my diary. I've been writing things down since the first year after the accident, when I took over the diary from my mother, who had kept it since the accident. This included hospital appointments as well as comments.

On 1 April, I had been doing too much again. I felt rough with dodgy guts, so I went to the doctor's. He diagnosed a stomach infection. After that I watched the aikido. I picked up a bit and learned a lot from just watching. I'm still learning by my mistakes to this day, as I did back in April 1996. I was doing far too much then and I had to learn about my body's capacity. I would overdo it and pay the price by being laid up. It was all a learning process. I had become interested in alternative medicine, as times they are a-changin', for the better. I'm going to be on this planet for 161 years, and my mind will live on forever. I know this as I'm learning about Buddhism. I became interested in Buddhism when the spirits drew me to chi kung.

I carried on in 1996 with aikido courses, and I continued overdoing it with very long walks. I had numerous instances of bad guts. I continued to practice on the computer to build up to writing this book. I went to the Natural Health Show up at the students' union, which was an eye-opener.

Chapter 3

At the end of December the only medication I was taking was Prozac. I had stopped with all the health tablets. I also took a cream base with cypress, myrrh, cedar wood, and frankincense, and I fasted twice a week, which kept me looking young. I was meditating for half an hour at a time, but I had a short break for Christmas in which I just did yoga from a tape. I restarted my regular meditation on 27 December 1998 half an hour. No swimming or aikido. I had four experiences whilst meditating:

1. I saw what looked like a mirage in the desert and space.
2. At the back of my mind, I saw what looked like mirrors flapping. I later found out when I told Len Sinclair about it that this was a mirage.
3. I experienced walking in space.
4. I had an experience like walking down an orange tunnel.

On Tuesday, 29 December 1998, I resumed my training, as I call it. I went for a swim up at Maindee, taking a taxi there and back. I meditated for half an hour. The previous three times I set my alarm clock for an hour and came up after half an hour. I had an experience of a lotus flower in my throat. I remember reading about that experience. I filled up my time by buying veg and fruit, especially grapes with pips, reading papers, listening to music, and watching sports.

I tried a faith healer, and he sat me in a chair and put his hands on my knees, and I felt a pulling sensation. This was a while ago; I went because my mother was pestering me to go. I went, not believing or disbelieving, but now I realize you've got to experience these things before making judgement, as it's all in the mind. Since the accident I've learned by my mistakes. I was one of the first to survive with my brain injury. Technology is so far advanced that they are even bringing people back from the dead (so to speak).

Time is going really, really fast, and it's now 3 January. I had a chi kung seminar up Ponthir (Newport) way. Len commented that I was walking a lot better. I put this down to not going for long walks anymore. He is now training me to walk very, very slowly, as he says it's all in the mind. I did this for a few weeks but forgot about it till the end of June. I have now started again. I also do the Feldenkrais method and have been reading about hypnotherapy. I met a practitioner down at the centre where I do my Feldenkrais method. I had a chat with Rick and told him about my accident and explained that I wanted to become soft and supple for aikido. I asked if hypnotherapy would help, and he said it would certainly speed things up, so I've got an appointment on 1 July 1999.

Everything I do is to improve my posture and mobility. This includes swimming, aikido, Feldenkrais, and now going to hypnotherapy. It's like my physio Debbie said when they got me on my feet: the rest is up to you. She said just after the accident that people with my sort of injury usually reach a plateau and stop improving. But I was determined not to let the brain injury beat me, so I did my exercises three times daily. I'll carry on improving till my dying day. I started having experiences whilst meditating, as I said earlier, and was gradually building to meditating half an hour three times daily, although at first I tried sitting longer. I was training over in Penarth for aikido from January until June on Mondays and at Peter Gillard's club up in Llanrumney. I would also swim twice a week up at Maindee. I was also fasting twice a week, on Sunday and Wednesday, and was having lots of experiences.

On 22 January I tried a different Buddhist meditation group, and I was getting closer to my three-times-daily meditation by the end of January. I also went to a Buddhist talk up in Bristol with Johnathon on a Wednesday. I fasted and still went by train and was fine. I knew I would be off course, as I'd been going places whilst fasting since the beginning. When I first fasted, I went to the sports centre. half an hour

I was going on my computer three times weekly for over an hour, but now I find that half an hour daily is fine. I was even overdoing it on the computer, and my brain would get all fuzzed up. I would press something on the computer, and Rob would have to come down to fix my mistakes.

In February nothing really happened except more Buddhist meetings up in Bristol. Whilst the kids were on holiday, I had a break too but found other ways to overdo it.

I turned thirty-six on 20 February and now I get my buzz from fruit and water. I met a woman in chi kung who had been to a Feldenkrais class and said she would send me details. I had been reading about this technique for years, and if you're meant to do something, it will happen for you. On Monday, 1 March 1999, I was lucky enough to find a book called *The Elusive Obvious* by Moshe Feldenkrais. I went to Bristol to pick up a meditation cushion.

It was now 5 March 5 1999, exactly ten years since the accident. I went to an instructors' course for aikido on Sunday, 7 March 1999 and handed in the work that I had done. I had sent a letter of to the Buqi College of Healing, but they wanted £400 for a week's course without accommodation. I had a phone call from Sofi, who was running the course, and I asked about accommodation, saying I'd sleep on her floor, but she said she had someone staying already. It would have been all right if I had somewhere to stay, but going away to London on my own was a bit dodgy, and the area where the course took place was rough.

Criss, a Buddhist that I met in chi kung a while ago, was coming to give me a talk on Buddhism. I had become interested in reiki healing, as it was covered in school courses. I didn't expect to pay much for something I already had; I just wanted to get into the circle, so to speak. I went on a reiki course at Severn Road on Saturday, 27 March, from 10.00 to 4.00 with Joan.

Thursday, April 1 1999. April went as normally for me as you might expect. I do weird things, so other people say, but to me they are normal for long life and health. I fasted on the 2nd and the 4th, Friday and Sunday. Friday was a bank holiday, so I watched rugby league and ate some raw veg. On the 10th and 11th, Saturday and Sunday, I was going to go train up at Newtown Spring Course, but I was ill about halfway there. I just went up and watched, as I wasn't right. I knew my own body, and it felt right to just watch. It's good to watch sometimes, as you pick up on things.

On Monday the 12th, I fasted and went to Penarth Dojo to watch the aikido. I was much better on the way home, although I didn't eat till I got home. I watched Wales beat England. I still had the slight tummy bug that I came down with whilst going to Newtown, but I found excuses like travel sickness and too much food before I travelled. I do suffer with my stomach. The doctor gave me antibiotics.

Wednesday, 14 April 1999. I met a woman called Romona whilst being picked up for chi kung. She was talking about Feldenkrais technique on 28 February. I went to the Parade Centre off Newport Road from 7.00 to 9.00 for a class with Darien Pritchard. The class went well. Four people were there. It cost £5 for a group lesson and £25 for a private lesson. I kept up my meditation but stopped my standing, as I overdid it as I always do. I went to aikido and had an injury to my the ligaments in my foot while falling awkwardly. Next day I had a massage from Len Sinclair at from 4.00 to 5.00. Rob the computer boffin came at 2.00, as I had pressed something again. I rested my foot for the weekend, as I had to, but it is not that easy to rest.

I went and watched the aikido up at Roath on Monday, 19 April 1999 to get out of the house.

On Wednesday, 21 April 1999, I had a private Feldenkrais appointment with Darien Pritchard, and I got much more out of the one-to-one session than a class. Next day I watched aikido up at Llanrumney. I thought the ligaments in my foot had healed, but I went up to Maindee for a gentle swim, thinking a swim would do it good, but I only banged my foot as I got in. I tried to do a bit, but it was not meant to be, so I got straight out. The spirits were telling me that I needed rest. Things like this always happen, so you've got to always look at the signs and do what feels right for you, as no two people are the same, no matter how many people tell you differently.

Saturday, 24 April 1999. Joan, the reiki teacher I had up at Severn Road, said there was a reiki share every fourth Saturday of the month up at Kymin, Beach Hill. I went out of interest to see her. It was all women laying their hands on others. I fasted, as was going to a chi kung seminar the next day. I kept up my meditation twice a day and also went swimming at Maindee. My foot was rested, so I went over to Penarth for aikido from 8.00 to 10.00. I practiced meditation at the same times, at 6.00 and last thing in the day, at this stage.

Tuesday, 27 April 1999. There was supposed to be a reiki class done at the adult education centre, but not enough people turned up: there were only four including me, and they needed eight to hold the class.

Wednesday, 28 April 1999. I had a private Feldenkrais technique session. Pritchard worked on my left side, as that was the side that was paralysed, and my hips. It was an excellent session, and I could feel myself loosening up. I was doing the Feldenkrais method every other week, and I could feel that I was improving and was told that as well. It was my well-advanced physiotherapy; my aikido is advanced physiotherapy.

I had a shiatsu appointment at the centre on 7 May 1999. I continued my meditation twice a day and my swimming. On Saturday the 8th I went to the Natural Health Show, which was very interesting. I went to various lectures, walked around the stalls, and without realizing it, I was drawn to reiki. I attended a talk and met a man working at a stall who was a reiki practitioner who told me a lot about it. So I arranged to go up to his house and do reiki. It went really well, but at this stage I was still searching for a healing method that was the best for me. The next day I went to chi kung up in Pentwyn. Next day was a swim up in Maindee and aikido over in Penarth. On 11 May I booked up for a Buddhist course with meditation. Len Sinclair said it was all right to go. That was when I listened to him and minded what he said, but now I realize that he's only in it for his own personal gain—i.e. money. I went to Severn Road on Wednesday the 12th for reflexology and aromatherapy then took a taxi up to Roath for my Feldenkrais appointment at 4.00. On Thursday the 13th, I did swimming up in Maindee, aikido in the evening, and three sessions of meditation.

I did reiki with at the students' union with Martain from Llandeyrn. I did reiki 1 one week and reiki 2 the following Friday. Things have happened so slowly it's a wonder I haven't given up, but you've just got to keep on going no matter what. I went to my second session with the Buddhist group up in St Peter's

Street on Monday after aikido and a swim. I continued with my meditation twice a day, at about 6.00 and last thing in the day and went to my aromatherapy and reflexology class in Severn Road. I went swimming the same day as aikido. I did this on and off ever since I can remember, as far back as when Empire Pool was still up, when I'd go to Channel View to the gym that has since been demolished. I took a taxi back home to Lula's (Mum's) and walked up to Empire Pool.

Friday, 22 May 1999. I did my reiki 2 attunement and was told I will know on my own when I'm ready for reiki 3. I had a free weekend from my courses. I treat my activities and classes as my job. It has been a very, very slow job, but I'm in no rush and have learned to pace myself. Rushing is what causes dis-ease and stress. I had a nice rest on the weekend watching sports.

Monday, 24 May 1999. I went for a swim up at Maindee Pool and could feel myself overdoing it again, so I just went and watched aikido over in Penarth. I just do chi kung exercises now, as I tend to overdo the standing postures.

On the 25th, I had a Buddhism course. This was my third week and was just basic Buddhism. On Wednesday the 26th I had a swim up at Maindee after having a massage by two women in aromatherapy and reflexology in Severn Road. I then left at about 3.00 and got a taxi to my Feldenkrais appointment, which went very well. I then had a taxi back home and had a bath and a kip. I woke up to watch Manchester United versus Bayern Munich and did three half-hour sessions of meditation. The next day I had aikido from 8.30 to 10.00 and had a swim up at Maindee. Friday I just took it easy with meditation. I had a good aikido session the night before. I always do, as any sort of training in which I get a sweat on gives me a buzz, but with aikido training, I also get results after all the time I put in. At this stage I was meditating three times daily when possible.

I had a chi kung session on Sunday, 30 May 1999. It was a very slow job, but it is for health and long life, so there's no need to rush it. I had been getting ready for the past week to go to Switzerland with aikido for the thirtieth anniversary celebration of Swiss aikido. Eight top Japanese practitioners and people from all over the world were going. I had a quiet few days before going to Switzerland on Friday morning. I went with Mike and a boy from Barry. I was picked up about 8.00 as we had to fly at 10.00 and had to be there a good half an hour before take-off. We then changed at Amsterdam and got a train from Zurich to where the aikido was being held. It was amazing to meet people of so many different nationalities. We did a lot of walking thinking we had a place to stay, but we ended up in an air-raid shelter that had been prepared for aikido people. It was a great course. I learned that weekend that everyone's learning and you should not only give but take as well. I didn't think much of the Swiss aikido, as by looking around, I could tell that Kanetsuka Sensei maintained very high standards in the UK. We left on Saturday night as we all had only one session on Sunday morning.

For the next few days after the Switzerland trip, I was really tired, so I took it easy Monday and Tuesday. I didn't go to the fifth Buddhist course, but I planned to go with Len Sinclair on a day trip to Raglan Tibetan Buddhist Centre on 19 June.

On Wednesday, 9 June 1999, I took it easy just filling in the time with constructive activities, such as aromatherapy and reflexology at Severn Road from 1.00 to 3.00. I then had a Feldenkrais appointment at 4.00 with Darien Pritchard at the centre and did two half-hour meditation sessions.

Thursday, 10 June 1999. After the weekend away in Switzerland without any meditation, I resumed Wednesday. I've started tripping, as I call it. Len Sinclair said that I was tripping, so after doing this diary, I'll give him a bell later and get some advice. I phoned Len up, and he said I was daydreaming and must practice single-mindedness, concentrating on an object or my breath. I count up to twenty-one, and if I get distracted, I go back to one and start again.

I'm went to my old routine of aikido Tuesdays and Thursdays and yoga Mondays for the next few weeks and was meditating three times a day when possible. I went to aikido in Penarth on Friday the 18th to help out.

Saturday, 19 June 1999. Len Sinclair had arranged a day trip to Lam Rim Buddhist Centre in Raglan. It went very well. I bought a few books on meditation. Things ambled along very slowly, but I was in no rush. After aromatherapy and reflexology at Severn Road, I worked very hard in Feldenkrais method, which is good. Pritchard is taking an interest in me, as he can see the improvement I'm making. He's working me all the harder, as I like being pushed. It's all in the mind; body and mind should be one.

No aikido on the Thursday, too knackered. Went Friday instead. I had a chi kung seminar on Sunday the 27th, so I fasted the Saturday before watching sports, Wales versus South Africa. We had our first ever victory over South Africa. I happened to view a film called *Kundun*, which I ordered not knowing what or who it was, but I feel I was drawn to it by the spirits.

I was carrying on with my meditation two or three times daily, but not with eyes open like Len Sinclair. About a month later I was meditating fine but not with eyes open. I started with ten-minute sessions and built up. I did this for a couple of days and was fine, so I meditated for half-hour sessions with eyes open. I'd gone through all the stages of meditation, including experiences, and knew I must carry out single-minded concentration. There is no wrong or right way to meditate. I carried on meditating twice a day for roughly half an hour and three or four times a day if I had the time.

I then went to a healing demonstration up at the centre with a psychic named Richard. The psychic healing was amazing, so I tried a weekend workshop with Richard, who was an associate of Alan Burnett, a reiki master. On the Saturday, Richard said, 'There's a person in this room who's holding a grudge against someone in this room.' I didn't think anymore about this, but the next day during a group therapy session at about 4.30, I volunteered for a particular thing going on, and it came out that I was a sorcerer in a previous life. The person who was holding a grudge was a girl I had cast a spell upon. She had a paralysis on her right side; mine was the left. Everything he said was making sense. He said that I was on a quest trying out therapies and that I still haven't found one for me but that I will.

I carried on with my routine, and on Wednesday, 7 July 1999, I had aromatherapy and reflexology from 1.00 to 3.00 at Severn Road and then a Feldenkrais appointment at 4.00 at the centre by Glan Hafren college. Darien Pritchard said he likes working with me, not just because he's taking my money but because he can see the improvement I'm making, and he sets me harder tasks to perform at every session. Tuesdays, Thursdays, and Fridays I had aikido and went swimming.

On Saturday, 10 July 1999, I tried a psychic awareness group led by Terry Davies who was a psychic and a crystal healer.

Sunday, 11 July 1999. I tried yet another therapy session run by Terry Davies about tarot cards, and it was crap. When I meditate, I do it twice a day religiously and sometimes maybe three times, with eyes open. I had to start my meditation over again, as Len said I was daydreaming and getting my mind all muddled up. I watch the breath and count to twenty-one, and if my mind wanders, I start again. I breathe in and out for the count of one, in and out for the count of two, and so on till I reach twenty-one. When I started reading, I'd try out certain things for myself, and then a short while later I'd read in a book that I was going about things right.

I went to an introduction to basic Buddhism meeting with chanting and it was well weird. I only went as it was across the road.

On Wednesday, 15 July, I went to see about a new Hawaiian huna place which was in an old hairdresser's. They did various therapies there, but I'd been there done that and got the jacket, so to speak.

Friday the 16th, I had an appointment with Dr Lloyd Byu, but he cancelled, so I went down to Lula's and then got picked up from there for aikido over in Penarth. Sunday I fasted. In aikido, I'm understanding the hips lately, and now I realize that everything comes from the hips and centre. Even a back bend. I thought that was the back bending, but now I know that it is the hips. Last time I trained, Russel, whom I was partnering at the time, said, 'Bend and use your hips.' It sank in then that when doing a back bend, the hips must bend. The improvement is so slow. I still notice a lot of people on the mat are avoiding me, black belts included. I just work with certain people I know and trust, Russel and a few others. But someone whom I thought I could depend on wasn't telling me certain things, such as when doing an application in which you go to the head with the arm. I was training with Gutren for application, and she stopped me and told me that I was going away from the head. Not to mention any names, but I later trained with someone doing the same application, and it came out later in the pub that I was going away from the head. I had a Hawaiian huna session up at Marcus Weast's house. It was interesting. He says there are three levels of the subconscious mind. It all boils down to the same goal: looking for long life. I am currently doing hypnotherapy at the centre but am of two minds whether to continue the sessions, as I think he's ripping me off.

Sunday, 18 July 1999. I've got to start my meditation over again, as Len said I had been daydreaming. I started my meditation again with eyes open, aiming for single-minded concentration.

Tuesday, 20 July 1999. I'm starting off with ten-minute sessions and will gradually build up.

I've started to do meditation with eyes open for three-quarters of an hour to get single-minded concentration. I did this for a few sessions, and then I read that I had been meditating right. Things like this have happened to me from the very beginning, as the Spirits are with me and guiding me on the right path.

Wednesday, 21 July 1999. I had a hypnotherapy session, dealing with the subconscious mind, from 3.00 till 4.00, and then a Feldenkrais session from 4.00 till 5.00 at the centre. My teacher, Darien Pritchard, is giving me more challenging exercises to do, as he can see the improvement. I was meditating twice a day, last thing and in daylight. By 22 July I was up to twenty-five minutes early and thirty-five minutes last thing, building up to two lots of forty-five minutes.

Friday, 23 July 1999. Ambled along filling in my time with productive activities, meditation, etc., and home for the rugby league at 7.00. At this stage I was doing a meditation visualizing a warm lubricant coming from my brain and flushing through my body, making all my muscles soft and supple. I had this idea from my hypnotherapy instructor at the centre, Rick. I fasted and had a chi kung seminar the next day. When Len Sinclair and I got talking and I mentioned a shiatsu course, he suggested that I do a foundation course to learn about the meridians, etc. I've already done one-day courses on shiatsu with Tony Penman.

Monday, 26 July 1999. I was doing two meditations for three-quarters of an hour and the third for various lengths. I planned to go away to aikido summer school Saturday, so I went to aikido Tuesday and had rest Thursday. I just went swimming three times and did my meditation. Once I get something in my brain I follow it through religiously. We set off for aikido summer school on Sunday, as Mike had family problems. It was a really good summer school; I improved enormously. I kept up my meditation for three-quarters of an hour last thing at night. When I got home I was shattered, so I gave myself a week off aikido and was able to have a gentle swim Thursday and Friday. I set my alarm for just over how long I have decided to sit, three-quarters of an hour, building up to twice a day eventually.

Chapter 4

Thursday, 5 January 2000. I've been learning Japanese since 27 September 1999. I started off going to have something to do, but the last couple of months I've been religiously studying for an hour or so, and I can now see the improvement. It's repetition: you've got to read over and over again, and words and sentences will come into your mind at weird times.

I had a dentist appointment at 2.00, so I got up earlyish and went swimming up at Maindee Pool, where I did my three-quarters of an hour. I do two lengths, stretch, and do the exercises Rick the hypnotherapist gave me. Then I took a taxi to the dentist at the Parade, where I'm having my bottom teeth done. I took a bus home from the dentist, had a bath, and relaxed all night watching Man United in the World Club Championship.

Friday, 7 January 2000. I fasted today, as I have a shiatsu foundation course Saturday and Sunday. Just went out for papers and grapes, wrote up my work on the word processor, and watched Swansea Rugby play Toulouse in the European Cup.

Saturday, 8 January 2000. The course went pretty well on Saturday, but I came home about 6.30 and there was footy on at 8.00, so I stayed up after having tea, but I could not kip in the night. Was rough the next day and didn't go to shiatsu on Sunday.

Monday, 10 January 2000. I was glad things were back to normal. I had Japanese tonight from 7.00 to 9.00. I phoned Tony Penman, the shiatsu practitioner, for some advice and told him I had nearly finished a shiatsu foundation course. I explained that I've tried many possibilities of becoming a healer, and he says shiatsu isn't for me and gave me an address and phone number of a natural body healer's, so I phoned them up and they are going to send me some information on courses coming up.

Tuesday, 11 January 2000. I kept up my swimming at Maindee the same day as aikido and did twenty-five minutes of meditation. I got a call from Severn Road, and they asked if I was going to continue with reflexology and aromatherapy. Yesterday I forgot all about it.

Wednesday, 12 January 2000. Today I remembered aromatherapy and reflexology at Severn Road from 1.00 to 3.00. I had booked a taxi to pick me up at 2.30 to take me to the Parade where I had a hypnotherapy session from 3.00 to 4.00 and Feldenkrais from 4.00 to 5.00. At the hypnotherapy session, the therapist looks at my walking. In an advanced physiotherapy session, the therapist stretched my hamstrings and other muscles with physio elastic. He noticed that I was shuffling my left leg, so after many experiments, he determined that one leg is shorter than the other. So now I might have to see a podiatrist if a longitudinal arch support doesn't work.

Darien Pritchard was well pleased with the progress that I had made and gave me new exercises to do. These are similar to what I've been doing but are done standing up. The improvement is very slow, but as he can see, I've been patient, and he realizes that I know this and that that's why I've improved. I've known this since the beginning, when learning to walk up and down with the physio's bars.

Thursday, 13 January 2000. I'm going to aikido over in Penarth tomorrow. I meditated for twenty minutes in daylight. I also phoned the natural body and spiritual healers to enquire about the package of information I sent away for. Tony Penman gave me the address. I've tried many healing techniques and will now try yet another one. When I enquired, they said they did courses and sent me information that will reach me by Saturday the 15th. This looks like it, but I've said that before. I fasted today as I have a chi kung seminar tomorrow, listened to CDs, watched rugby, and generally filled the time.

Sunday, 16 January 2000. I was up early, at 8.45, in plenty of time to be picked up at 11.20. I did my ablutions and had bath after brekkie.

Next day I went to go to the Queens Arcade to the shoe shop for a longitudinal arch support. So I was up pretty early for me. I had a terrible night and awoke at 6.00 and then just dozed till 10.00. I had a taxi to the market and walked through to the Queens Arcade to get the arch support, which cost £19.95. If this is not sufficient support, I'll go back to Dr Lush, who said he would book me in to Llandough to see a podiatrist on the NHS.

Maybe there'll be a bit of a wait, but it's better than paying in excess of £200. I had aromatherapy and reflexology from 1.00 to 3.00 at Severn Road and then went back to the flat. After getting myself fed, as I realize how important food is since the accident, I got ready for Japanese.

Tuesday, 18 January 2000. I swim twice a week, on a the same day as aikido, Tuesdays and a Thursday or Friday, depending on what courses I'm doing on the weekend. I did my usual swim on a Tuesday the last two weeks, and since Christmas break, I've swum eight lengths each of freestyle, breaststroke, and backstroke with a bit of stretching, which takes me just under three-quarters of an hour, and I feel better for it. I'm preparing myself for a very long life by getting my teeth done and doing everything with the intent of not rushing. There's no rush. Everything is happening at the right time for my improvement. I am being looked after by my spirit.

Wednesday, 19 January 2000. I usually don't eat on Wednesdays unless I've got Feldenkrais with Darien Pritchard, but this Wednesday I just had aromatherapy and reflexology at Severn Road. I phoned Rick the hypnotherapist about the arch support, and he said, 'See how you get on with it till Wednesday the 26th,' my next appointment. At the moment I'm getting on fine with it. The massage course got cancelled, as there were not enough people. I'll just have aromatherapy and reflexology with Caroline at Severn Road.

Thursday, 20 January 2000. I went swimming up at Maindee and did my twenty-four lengths in just under three-quarters of an hour, stretching after each set of freestyle, backstroke, and breaststroke and finishing with a stretch. I was picked up by a taxi driver who hadn't picked me up for two months, and he noticed a big all-around improvement. There's a difference in attitudes among people, I find. I come across people all the time who just don't like the way I'm living. Got ready after swimming and tea a lie down for aikido. I did my Feldenkrais exercises twice today and meditation once.

Friday, 21 January 2000. I went to Splott Pool to see Barry, a lifeguard who used to help me a lot with advice on swimming and who coached me by giving me tips. I went there on the way to my mother's to get ready for aikido in Penarth. I don't usually go swimming and do aikido three times a week, and I paid the price on the weekend; I felt very tired.

Saturday, 22 January 2000. I had a quiet day. I had a small bet, as there was no rugby on live till 5.30. I was feeling very lethargic having gone swimming and done aikido three times this week. I was told by four different people how relaxed and loose I was, and my mobility has improved enormously. So I'll have to keep my aikido and swimming to twice a week, doing both on the same day.

Sunday, 23 January 2000. I have been fasting for six years and five months and feel better for it, as I have a good rest on weekends to get ready for my onslaught starting tomorrow. There's rugby on at 2.30, so I'll get ready for that rather than dig in the archives.

Monday, 24 January 2000. I've been overdoing it yet again. After doing my aikido and swimming three times in one week instead of my usual two, I've decided to have a long overdue rest from swimming and aikido. I was very tired over the weekend, kipping a lot. I've finished with aromatherapy and reflexology, as they are going over the same things yet again and I was only going for a back massage. It did me good and I know I'll move on to the next chapter in my improvement, but what that is, I don't know. I saw a programme that said that people who have had brain injuries have psychic abilities. I think that is very true, as I always knew I'd have the accident and do everything I'm doing at the moment. I also I used to have dreams about racehorses, and they would come in at ridiculously long odds.

Tuesday, 25 January 2000. A lady from the Lord Chancellor's office came today at 10.15, so I was up earlyish to do everything I had to do except eat. I had brekkie when she'd gone. She stayed for about half an hour. I was still feeling tired, so it was good timing that I had a week off from my normal routine, except for hypnotherapy with Rick for mobility exercises with physio's elastic.

Thursday, 27 January 2000. I had a dentist appointment to have a lower bridge and fillings done. I woke up at 2.30 for a pee and couldn't go back off after reading. I've been in bed at 10.30

or thereabouts every night after making the mistake of doing three lots of swimming and aikido.

Friday, 28 January 2000. I fasted today, doing what I used to do two or three years ago, and I could see the improvement I've made.

Saturday, 29 January 2000. I had a shiatsu foundation course, this weekend being the penultimate one, as I have the last one on the 12th and 13th. I did my Feldenkrais exercises. I have improved so much that I go straight to the last part for five minutes a few times a week when I have the time.

Monday, 31 January 2000. Rob the computer whizz-kid came at 1.00, and I had Japanese from 7.00 to 9.00. In the afternoon I went to Severn Road to enrol in a few courses. I also have a brochure for Vision for Living, the Natural Health Show, for February and am deciding what to do.

Chapter 5

Friday, 3 March 2000. Had a quiet day. I was ready for a long overdue rest. Super League kicks off tonight with Bradford Bulls versus St Helens at 7.30.

Saturday, 4 March 2000. I was going to fast, but I ate at 4.00, as I had to meet a bint at 7.00 at the Chapter Arts across the road. She was a dancer and we both have full lives, but nothing came of it. When I told her I was writing my memoirs, she recommended that I help others who have had bad accidents by writing a book aimed as a help for the general public.

Sunday, 5 March 2000. I had a bad session with Len Sinclair and can see that he's only in it for the money.

Monday, March 6 2000. I have an aikido course coming up next weekend and had chi kung this weekend, so I was going to fast, but I felt giddy when went for the paper, so I listened to my body and ate. I went swimming today to fit everything in, as I've got to swim and do aikido twice a week. I went to Lula's after swimming up at Maindee and then took a taxi at 6.30 to my Japanese lesson at Cantonian High School in Fairwater.

Tuesday, 7 March 2000. I continued with my meditation twice a day and was going to do aikido and swimming, but I swam yesterday. I gave aikido a miss as I have a course on the weekend and fasted today.

Wednesday, 8 March 2000. I had a Feldenkrais appointment from 4.00 to 5.00 at the Parade. I saw Kelly down at the health shop. We still go out occasionally, but we both have our time full up.

Thursday, 9 March 2000. I went trout fishing up at Cefn Mably Lakes. I had no luck, but it was enjoyable. A taxi driver who hasn't picked me up for about six weeks picked me up from Cefn Mably and noticed a big improvement. He said I'm a right little action man, as he's taken me swimming and to aikido.

Friday, 10 March 2000. I went fishing at Cefn Mably but had no luck. I was going to go on an aikido course the 11th and 12th, so I gave Penarth a miss. I was feeling well overtired, a warning not to train on the weekend, so I listened to my body.

Monday, 13 March 2000. I fasted last Tuesday as I was busy Wednesday, and you need food. I was also overtired this weekend, so I ate. Fasting today makes it my second fast for the week. Rob—the computer whizz-kid came at 11.00 to have a look at my word processor, as it was going funny. If Rob can't do it, no one can. He fixed it, and it went back to normal. The last few days I've not been sleeping. I put this down to my wanting to train weekends, but aikido is such a slow job, and I need a rest on weekends to recharge my batteries. After Rob came, I had a taxi to the dentist, then to Lula's, and then to Japanese at 6.30 for the lesson from 7.00 to 9.00 at Cantonian High School Fairwater.

Tuesday, 14 March 2000. I try to keep my aikido and swimming to twice a week. I saw Kelly down at the health shop.

Wednesday, 15 March 2000. I fasted today. Monday's fast was from last week, so this week I've just got to fast Wednesday and Saturday or Sunday to make it twice. Saw Kelly down at the health shop, and we're going to arrange to go out again.

Thursday, 16 March 2000. I did my usual swim up at Maindee and aikido from 8.30 to 10.00. We had a good session today, as there were a lot of beginners there, and Peter Gillard says the way to progress is to practice with beginners. Everyone is a beginner, as everyone is improving. Peter Gillard asked me to go to Penarth Dojo tomorrow.

Friday, 17 March 2000. I still haven't been sleeping too well, so I stoked up my fruit and got ready for another onslaught. Went to Maindee Pool with my aikido bag, had a swim, and went by taxi to Lula's. I watched a few aikido videos then had a taxi at 7.45 to Arcot Street Church, where I did aikido. I have a cold, the first one since I can remember. I've had the sniffles now and again, but this one is bordering on being fluey. So I tried to carry on with my routine and decided to go swimming for a third time this week and do aikido over in Penarth to try to sweat it out. Also, I did my Feldenkrais exercises for a third time this week. A number of people commented on the progress I am making, so I think my routine is paying off.

Saturday, 18 March 2000. I had a lucky fifteen, a 20 to 1 winner, all on the telly, out of interest, and then I settled down for Wales versus Scotland.

Sunday, 19 March 2000. The cold has thickened up a lot today, but I'll eat today, as you starve a fever but feed a cold. The last few weeks I've been fasting Mondays and Wednesdays due to busy weekends, and I've got another full weekend with an iridology course at Severn Road on 25 March and an aikido course from 10.00 to 3.00 on the 26th.

Monday, 20 March 2000. My cold has gone stuffy, but it is okay. I went over to Tesco at 11.00 for fruit. I went down Lula's in the afternoon and took a taxi from there to Japanese at Cantonian High School.

Tuesday, 21 March 2000. The cold was a lot better today, and I couldn't stay in doing nothing even being a bit under par, so I decided to go to the sports centre for a swim. I had to renew my membership, as I haven't been there for about two years, and they have got a variety of different things to do.

Wednesday, 22 March 2000. I fasted today, making it my second time for the week, and I went to the dentist to get all my teeth sorted out. I've spent nearly £4,000. Saw Kelly down at the health shop, and we arranged to go out this Saturday.

Thursday, 23 March 2000. I went down the sports centre for a swim and did aikido from 8.30 to 10.00.

It was a terrible, rainy day, so you've got to keep busy making sure you've always got things to do and places to go. That's why I keep a diary. I've kept it since the accident, taking over the one my mother used to keep for hospital appointments. The improvement is so slow that close family don't really notice it, but someone who only sees me, say, once a month notices a big improvement. I still get told to this day by various different people, mostly taxi drivers who pick me up every couple of months, that they notice a big difference. I'm starting to go back down to the sports centre after an eighteen-month layoff. I had been going to Maindee o swim instead, but looking back, I should have kept going to the sports centre, as there are plenty of people about.

Friday, 24 March 2000. I took it easy in the daytime, going to Tesco, the health shop, and to aikido over in Penarth. That makes it three times that I've trained, Tuesday, Thursday, and Friday. I'm supposed to go on a course Sunday, but after Saturday's iridology at Severn Road, I didn't realize I had a course till I looked at my diary whilst having brekkie. I got myself ready without rushing and was an hour late. It went well and was a day out. I then took Kelly to see a film in the Chapter Arts. The last few weeks I've given meditation a rest, but I've been reading about how beneficial meditation is and how the subconscious mind plays a big part in it. I started off sitting for fifteen minutes with eyes open. The last few weeks I've fasted Monday and Wednesday, so I fasted Monday, 27 March, and went along to my Japanese class. It went excellently. After a week's rest from learning, repetition, and reading over and over again, I answered quite a few questions.

Tuesday, 28 March 2000. I went swimming to the sports centre. There is much more to see and to do there if you want. I then got my food prepared and got ready for my aikido, which was from 8.00 to 10.00 in Plasnewydd Community Hall. Food takes up a lot of my time, as I need good plenty of fruits and vegetables, liver or chicken. I also meditated for fifteen minutes.

Wednesday, 29 March 2000. I was fasting today. I kept busy by cashing money from the post office, shopping over at Tesco for papers and odds and ends. I've been able to go out walking around since I first started fasting.

Thursday, 30 March 2000. I went for a short walk to Chapter Arts after getting the papers to enquire about the shamanic Indian dancing. It would help my balance. I heard about it from Kelly. I went for a swim up at the sports centre, got my grub ready, and then got ready for aikido.

Friday, 31 March 2000. I had a dentist appointment at 10.30 with Wyn Jenkins at the Parade. I'm having my teeth all done, as I'm going to be around for 161 years or thereabouts. Wyn Jenkins said my teeth will probably outlast my body when I told him how long I would be on this planet. I saw Kelly down at the health shop. We are both busy all the time, she with her dancing and me with my aikido and Japanese and other activities, so we see each other when appropriate. I went to aikido from 8.00 to 10.00 in Penarth at Arcot Street Church. It was a good session tonight, as I had sword-work practice with Sensei Peter Gillard, who has taken an interest in me from the beginning.

Saturday, 1 April 2000. Watched Wales beat Ireland and got ready for night, a I went to see Japanese drummers in St David's

Hall with about six others from aikido, including Sensei Peter Gillard. Afterwards we went to a pub in town.

Sunday, 2 April 2000. I ate today, as I had already fasted twice, and watched sports most of day. I meditated twice for half an hour and once for twenty minutes and prepared food.

Monday, 3 April 2000. I fasted today and will Friday this week as I have commitments Wednesday with Feldenkrais at 6.00. I'm seeing Kelly at 2.30 to go out somewhere, as we are both busy this weekend. I have Japanese from 7.00 to 9.00 at Cantonian High School.

Tuesday, 4 April 2000. I went to the sports centre for a swim and did aikido from 8.30 to 10.00 at Plasnewydd Community Hall and did twenty minutes of meditation last thing, as my day was full and only had time last thing.

Wednesday, 5 April 2000. Saw Kelly and went over to Chapter Arts at 3.00 after she'd finished work. I then had a Feldenkrais appointment at 6.00 and watched a footie match, Chelsea in Europe, and again did twenty minutes of meditation last thing.

Thursday 6 April 2000. I had a swim up at the sports centre, where we were organizing lifts for a course in Newtown, but only a few are going, so I'll have to find out Friday night over in Penarth. Did aikido from 8.00 to 10.00. I've started going to the sports centre for a swim rather than Maindee, as the sports centre gives out a sheet every two weeks saying what times the pool is available, and these times suited me. Before I stopped going as their times weren't convenient, sometimes from 10.00 to 11.00, and I was happy going to Maindee, as times were more flexible, from 6.00 a.m. to 10.00 p.m. I did half an hour's meditation in the afternoon.

Friday, 7 April Friday 2000. I was fasting today and trying to get a lift to Newtown.

Saturday, 8 April 2000. Restful weekend but can't keep still. I did a lot of walking today. I took a taxi to the market, walked to Spiller's, where I bought some CDs, walked back to St David's Hall to see Asian dancers, then back to the market where I bought second-hand records, some of which were collectors' items. Then I went down to Colin's, and we watched the rugby at his flat in Westgate Street. Cardiff beat Edinburgh Reivers. After the match

I walked to Lula's for tea and took a taxi home. I then did ten minutes of Feldenkrais exercises (I've improved enormously) and settled down after music at 8.30 for boxing.

Sunday, 9 April 2000. I had to see Len Sinclair about my ribs. They were playing me up. I did something in aikido, but I didn't pull up in agony, so I thought it must be a sprain or something like that. I've torn the muscle between the ribs called the intercostal muscle, and it's giving me terrible gyp. When I first did it last week, I was aggravating it by going swimming, and it was not healing.

Monday, 10 April 2000. Saw Kelly at 3.00 and took her to Chapter Arts and went to my Japanese class from 7.00 to 9.00 at Cantonian High School. The class broke up today till 8 May; went pretty well. Meditated for fifteen minutes.

Tuesday, 11 April 2000. I had a podiatric appointment at 10.00, and I had a rest from aikido due to another injury. I always learn too late, but everything happens for a reason. The reason for this is that I was rolling awkwardly. I angled my head to look behind me and just rolled very badly. I could have done myself more permanent damage.

Wednesday, 12 April 2000. Fasting today. I meditated for twenty-five minutes. I swam Monday and Tuesday, and today I realized I was doing myself more harm than good by not giving my muscles time to heal.

Thursday, 13 April 2000. I had to rest from aikido, but I kept to the same routine by watching, which was very difficult to do, but, alas, I had to rest my shoulder.

Friday, 14 April 2000. As the week went on, my shoulder was getting progressively worse, so I phoned Len Sinclair. He asked If I'd been to the doctor's, which was the last option I'd considered. I was down at Mum's when I phoned him, so I then made an emergency appointment with a doctor, as the pain was that bad, and Dr Lloyd saw me at 4.30. He put me on tablets and said I had strained the muscle going down the side of my back and told me to rest completely for ten to fourteen days. It's very difficult for me to stay still for even five minutes unless I've got a rugby match or a good film to watch.

Saturday, 15 April 2000. I went over to Chapter Arts in the afternoon.

On Sunday, 16 April 2000, I had to eat, as I was on tablets must be taken with food, and I went to Cousins Mariner's baby's christening.

Monday, 17 April 2000. I had a three-week holiday from Japanese, as schools were closed. Saw Kelly down at the health shop and arranged to take her out on Saturday to a Japanese restaurant. My back is still giving me gyp, but I can't keep still. Did a bit of Japanese for an hour and read my notes. I've got to try to keep my routine going as near as possible without doing actual aikido and swimming.

Tuesday, 18 April 2000. I'll keep to my routine and go to watch aikido training, with Mum coming in the afternoon. My course of tablets finish on a bank holiday, Monday the 24th.

Wednesday, 19 April 2000. Cashed money and went to see Kelly at the health shop. The tablets I'm on are called ibuprofen, and the bottle specifies that I should take one with food three times daily. I think I had this injury to slow me down, as every holiday I get a slight injury, telling me to rest. I've learned to rest at weekends unless there's an aikido or chi kung course, and then I'll fast and have a complete rest on the Friday before. I fast twice a week, usually Sunday and Wednesday, but I'll swap my days over to make sure I fast twice a week.

Thursday, 20 April 2000. I was going to go and train in aikido, but I'd be doing more harm than good. I did a bit of light stretching at tea-time and then got my bag ready and was all set to go up, and I'm writing this on the computer at 6.30. I had a bath after stretching and felt like training, but it's a weird injury, a tear in the muscle. My tablets finish on Monday, so I'll get back into it lightly then. It's impossible not training or swimming, but I've been overdoing it other ways.

Friday, 21 April 2000. This is a big rugby weekend, with New Zealand versus Australia at 10.30 and then Wigan versus St Helens. I'll tape these matches. Last night was Wakefield versus Castle for rugby league, and today I'm going to watch Cardiff versus a Scottish side and go down to Mum's for tea and then home to watch what I taped.

Saturday, 22 April 2000. I bought a ticket for Ebbw Vale versus Llanelli and Swansea versus Pontypridd costing £15 at the Millennium Stadium. It was a great experience. There were three tiers, and it looks empty from the telly, but there are three bars. Everyone queues up to be served, and you can watch the match and drink. Not that I touch the demon drink; I just took my isotonic drink and bananas, grapes, and bread with a piece of chicken.

Sunday, 23 April 2000. Today was the last day of the tablets prescribed by Dr Lloyd for my shoulder, and this week I've eaten, as you have to take them with food. I meditated for twenty-five minutes once a day for the last couple of days.

Monday, 24 April 2000. I was fasting today, as my tablets finished yesterday. I've been advised by Len Sinclair to take it easy and not go to aikido but to do some very light stretching. I'll keep to my training but do no movement with my shoulder, just my lower body.

Tuesday, 25 April 2000. I was up pretty early for me, at 8.30, although I'm not training. I needed to go to town to shop like my old routine and see a few people. I needed a break from training, and it took an injury. Every time there's a holiday, something happens to make me rest. Got home about 2.30 and made some veg and tea. Then I went and watched aikido at Plasnewydd Community Hall. It's surprising the things you pick up by just watching.

Chapter 6

Wednesday, 26 April 2000. I phoned Tom for a lift to chi kung Sunday, 30 April. Len Sinclair advised me not to go to the Natural Health Show on Sunday to see two healers, saying they would only take my energy and that I should stick to chi kung. We do a bit of chi kung healing at seminars, but he is biased towards chi kung.

Thursday, 27 April 2000. I didn't go swimming or to aikido, resting my side. I trained in aikido lightly but put myself back to the beginning.

Friday, 28 April 2000. It was the third time this week that I fasted, making up for last week when on tablets. I listened to my body and knew that I couldn't go swimming or do aikido. I'll have to let my side heal. I now know that it's a tear in the muscle, and that's going to take a long time to heal. The computer wouldn't save, so Rob the computer whizz-kid came down.

Saturday, April 29 2000. The Natural Health Show was today. I went to a talk with Soozi Holbeche which was very interesting. One of the things she said was about UFOs. I was a bit taken aback by this, as everything I had said a few years ago was coming true, and she reckons we'll make contact in some shape or form in the near future. I then went around to all the stalls. I bought many things, including an Aborigine didgeridoo, and carried them all home to the flat without pain. I then went to chi kung the following day and was in terrible pain on occasion. Len advised me not to do aikido, but I'll listen to my own body. Chi kung was a bit too much.

Monday, 1 May 2000. I had a quiet day. I watched rugby league and decided to have break from aikido.

Tuesday, 2 May 2000. My side is fine. I was going to have a rest from aikido and swimming; I think I deserve a rest. I fasted three times last week, Monday, Wednesday, and Friday.

Wednesday, 3 May 2000. My side was playing me up again in certain positions and movements.

Thursday, 4 May 2000. Made an appointment with Dr Lush, and he put me on another course of ibuprofen, which thins the blood around the affected area. With rest, it should heal.

Friday, 5 May 2000. It's the third week off aikido and swimming. It's the intercostal muscle between the ribs.

I rested over the weekend. It was very difficult to do nothing. I had a rest from chi kung, as that's what I think did my side in. I'm still carrying things all the time and putting myself back to the beginning. I've been off now for four weeks and am treating it as a well-deserved rest. Everything happens for a reason, the reason being that I was doing too much as usual, and the weather is getting hotter and the brain doesn't like the heat.

Wednesday, 10 May 2000. Since 1 January 2000 I've been drinking my urine in a glass poured from my bottle. First I'd be tempted to drink my urine when emptying my bottle for a couple of months, and then I finally plucked up enough courage to drink it. At first, I'd pour the wee into a small glass. I continued doing this till I increased my urine intake to exactly half a pint, or two glasses of pee.

Thursday, 11 May 2000. Continued to rest from aikido because of the injury but kept up my leg work and light stretching so I won't be too much out of it when I finally go back.

Friday, 12 May 2000. I was meant to go on a kum nye healing weekend up at Lam Rim Buddhist Centre the 12th, 13th, and 14th but had to cancel because I would only be putting more pressure on my side by carrying bags. Rob the computer whizz-kid came at noon. I have lost about a month's work (not the first time). I then had bought a ticket to see *Ghost Dog: The Way of the Samurai* at the Chapter Arts at 6.00. I put the tape in to tape the rugby league, but I cocked up the second half somehow.

Saturday, 13 May 2000. I walked down to Lula's and did a bet, as I had nothing to do to occupy me, but then Julie and Steven came down and I went shopping over at the bay with them. Side okay in spells.

Sunday, 14 May 2000. I'm up to one and a half glasses of urine. They said in Rookie that I'd be doing strange things, but this takes the biscuit. I tried meditation, but my side was too painful.

Monday, 15 May 2000. I did aromatherapy and reflexology at Severn Road from 1.00 to 3.00 and Japanese from 7.00 to 9.00. I'll do myself more harm than good by going swimming, so I'll wait a bit longer before going.

Tuesday, 16 May 2000. I fasted Sunday and was going to again today but decided to eat at 2.30, as I need food to rebuild the muscle. I had a back massage in aromatherapy and reflexology, and my side was okay. I kept to my days of going out to watch aikido and have been watching a lot of tapes.

Wednesday, 17 May 2000. I am up to one pint of urine a day, four small glasses. I had no pain till night-time for two days.

Thursday, 18 May 2000. I had been off swimming for five weeks and decided to go and just use my legs with a float. On the way in I spoke to a sports-injury specialist who said that I should swim, and if it gave me pain, to get out. I was fine on my back, so I just did a bit: four on my back, two freestyle, two backstroke, and two breaststroke, taking half an hour. After that I was chuffed. I didn't push my luck by doing aikido and just watched.

Friday, 19 May 2000. I've cut my urine intake down to a glass in the morning after opening my bowels and a glass last thing at night, making it a total of half a pint of piddle a day. I was drinking a lot more urine, but I was peeing all the time. I've been swimming twice now with no ill effects except that my side feels tired at night. I've got an appointment with Dr Lush on Thursday, 25 May, as he is going to arrange physio for me.

Saturday, 20 May 2000. I had a busy day today. Went over to Chapter Arts, took a taxi to Lula's for a haircut from Julie before going to the match at 2.00 for the 3.00 kick-off of the Challenge Cup final between Llanelli and Swansea. Llanelli won. Then I walked down to Rose's for tea and took a taxi home. I then went to the sports centre for a half-hour swim.

Sunday, 21 May 2000. Day of rest. I meditated three-quarters of an hour and am going back to fasting twice a week now, as three times in previous weeks was a bit much. I've learned by my mistakes, as I have done all along.

Monday, 22 May 2000. My urine intake is down to one glass every morning. I had a busy day with a taxi to my podiatry appointment at 11.00 in Western Avenue. I then had a taxi to Maindee Baths. My side is healing fine, but I'm just taking it slow, as a tear is difficult to judge. You have to listen to your own body. They'll send for me in September. I took a taxi then to Severn Road for reflexology and aromatherapy. Caroline had mixed me up a mixture of camomile, ginger, and black pepper for my side as I asked her to last week. I walked back to the flat, sorted out my munchies, and got ready for Japanese at Cantonian High. I took a taxi their and got lift home, making it a total of five taxis for the day.

Tuesday, 23 May 2000. I cashed my money and went swimming. I'm getting stronger and stronger, but I'll leave out aikido for another week and go back 1 June. I've been doing a bit of strengthening of my legs in the water and postures in and out of the water so I won't be too bad when I go back. I've got a doctor's appointment Thursday about having physio. My side still gives me gyp in the evening, so I think I'll listen to the doctor's advice, as I have never had a tear in my muscle before, and these things take much longer to heal than other injuries.

Wednesday, 24 May 2000. Not eating today. I've gone back to fasting twice a week, Sunday and Wednesday. I'm getting myself prepared for my return to aikido. All being well, I'll go back the day after the bank holiday on 1 June.

Thursday, 25 May 2000. I saw Dr Lush at 4.40. I was going to have a swim and go straight to the doctor's by taxi, but I got a taxi from my flat and told the driver 4 Merches Gardens, Grangetown, instead of sports centre. I wasn't meant to go swimming. Dr Lush put me on a waiting list for physio and said to go back into training when my body feels ready. I've let the tear in my muscle heal for four weeks with a few minor setbacks. I went swimming and then went to watch aikido, and I got the urge to train, so I trained in my waterproof bottoms and vest and was okay.

Friday, 26 May 2000. I was tired after training yesterday. I don't want my brain to go backwards. I decided not to do swimming, as I've been four times this week, but now I'll go back to swimming twice a week, Tuesday and Thursday, the same as aikido, as I don't want to go overdoing things again. I'm going over to Chapter Arts in the afternoon for an hour and am going to see *The Long Good Friday* tonight at 6.15. I'll tape the rugby league and watch it when I get back, as I've got a full weekend of rugger.

Saturday, 27 May 2000. I bought a ticket for Wales versus the French Barbarians at Millennium Stadium. Kick-off was at 5.30. They were also showing the European Cup final between Munster and Northampton, which in my opinion was a more intense match. I then went down Lula's and had tea and couldn't get a taxi home because of the rain, so I stayed the night.

Sunday, 28 May 2000. I had put my fasting down to twice a week, Sunday and Wednesday, and am better for it. I meditated for thirty-five minutes.

Monday, 29 May 2000, a bank holiday. I went swimming at the sports centre, and I stayed in the water for forty-five minutes doing my new routine. I then walked home. Rugby league was on at 5.30, so I decided to have a bet for the bank holiday. I had my usual one winner in a lucky fifteen, Yankee at 5 to 1. I also priced a winner at 11 to 2 on telly but was too late for it.

Tuesday, 30 May 2000. I was aching a bit due to swimming and took it easy all day, waiting for aikido from 8.00 to 10.00 at Plasnewydd Community Hall. My side has been fine except for a bit of pain, but you can't have it all your own way. No pain no gain.

Wednesday, 31 May 2000. Today I was fasting and catching up with my video tapes and playing music. I also wrote a letter to a Miss Williams after several phone calls enquiring about an ad in the *South Wales Echo* about a healing workshop with Shakti Gawain being held at the Moat House Hotel, Llandeyrn, Cardiff. It kept me busy for an hour making phone calls and writing a letter.

Thursday, 1 June 2000. I'm trying out a new routine now and not going swimming the same day as aikido but still keeping it up twice a week. I felt better for it last week, as the brain gets tired. Had aikido at Llanrumney Leisure Centre from 8.30 to 10.00.

Friday, 2 June 2000. I was too tired after doing a third-kyu grading last night in aikido. Peter Gillard had asked me to bring my membership to check I was paid up to date. I got to aikido knowing that there were gradings for six and five, but I didn't know he was going to grade me and Brian, but I had a sneaky feeling. First we went through six, five, and four, and then I passed third kyu. I was too tired to go swimming because the grading took a lot out of me. I was glad it was sprung on me or else I'd have been kept awake thinking about it.

In the night I went to a Buddhist lecture at Insole Court opposite Rookward Hospital. I'd never heard of it before, and the taxi driver didn't know it either.

Saturday, 3 June 2000. I went to the following two days of the Buddhist retreat, as Saturday and Sunday gave instruction on meditation and exercises. No fasting this weekend; I'll do it tomorrow.

Monday, 5 June 2000. I was really tired after the weekend. I did a fruit fast today. I was up at 11.00 and went to get my fruit. They had a bargain over at Lora's, more than two boxes of grapes for £6. Then I went over to Tesco for the rest, as it is fresher. I was ready for reflexology and aromatherapy from 1.00 to 3.00 at Severn Road. I had a massage in the first part of the lesson and was really tired, so I went home for a lie down before I got ready for Japanese at Cantonian High School from 7.00 to 9.00.

Tuesday, 6 June 2000. I stated earlier that I'd go swimming different days to training, but that would be going backwards, as I had come to the right balance of swimming and training in aikido the same day. I stayed in the pool for half an hour, and that is just right. Any more and I get too tired. I walked back from the sports centre and could feel myself getting looser and looser. I got ready for aikido at Plasnewydd Community Hall from 8.00 to 10.00.

Wednesday, 7 June 2000. I was fasting today. I went over to Chapter Arts and did a bit of writing in Japanese out the back. Emma Langton, who I've known for years and see up at Buddhist meetings, was in Rookie in 1995 with a blood clot, which left her partially sighted. She told me about this brain-injured-people do and said she would send my name and address to Headway. I phoned up Headway and found out it's for doctors to find out more about the brain, but I don't think they will, not in my lifetime, anyway. There's a connection with the other side and UFOs, as aliens are far more advanced than we are. I thought I was going crazy-aid bonkers till I went to a talk with Soozi Holbeche up the students' union, and she said the same things, so things are all coming together lately.

Thursday, 8 June 2000. I was giving aikido a miss tonight and going to see healer, Shakti Gawain, who was doing a mini workshop at the Moat House Hotel, Llandeyrn, Cardiff, from 7.00 to 10.00 at a cost of £15, or £18 on the door. I went swimming in the afternoon at the sports centre.

Friday, 9 June 2000. I had a taxi to Rookie then a taxi to the sports centre, but I was too late, so I had a taxi straight to Lula's. I had tea, watched some tapes, and played some music and was feeling quite rough, so I phoned up the sports centre. They were open from 8.00 to 10.00, so I had at taxi home to the flat and then phoned another taxi to pick me up at 7.30. As I remember, when I was rough down at Lula's, I'd always go for a swim to the Empire Pool, as it was so handy, and Bernard Chezney, the trainer for the Paralympics, said swimming was an excellent therapy for the brain. I found this out for myself and used to go there as it was so handy.

Saturday, 10 June 2000. I had a restful weekend with the rugby league from last night in the afternoon, tea, then a film over at Chapter Arts from 6.15 to 8.00, and then home to watch the boxing.

Sunday, 11 June 2000. Another day of rest. I fasted for another day making, it twice this week, at this stage, Sunday and Wednesday. I watched rugby league from 6.00 to 8.00, a tape of rugby league, and had a bet.

Monday, 12 June 2000. I did a bit of phoning around looking for Bernard Chezney. Aromatherapy and reflexology at Severn Road from 1.00 to 3.00. Back home, I watched more rugby league and got my tea ready and got myself organized for Japanese from 7.00 to 9.00 at the Canton Pub. I did swimming today for fifty minutes and could feel myself overdoing it like I did in the past, so I'll go back to swimming the same day as aikido for only half an hour.

Tuesday, 13 June 2000. I went over to Chapter Arts to do my Japanese and had a rest from the sports centre but did aikido at 8.00 to 10.00. A few times I've tried to do my swimming on different days, but then I can't fit my swimming in, and it's important that I do. I had a lapse by treating swimming as a free day, but that's going backwards. I'm still learning by my mistakes, as I have done since the beginning.

Wednesday, 14 June 2000. I had a letter from Martin McGovern at the Court of Protection, as I have applied to handle my own money. I've now got to send another form off. He said, 'I am pleased to inform you that the court is willing to accept Dr Lush's medical evidence as sufficient to restore you to your own property and financial affairs.' I had to fill in an ODP 6, which they sent me. I went to the Headway AGM meeting up at Rookie, as I have finally decided to help others. There are a few people up there with brain injuries, and even though their injuries aren't as severe as mine, they are worse off than I am. I've been very lucky, as I always knew I'd have the accident, and I've fought it from the very beginning, learning by my mistakes all along. It went all right. I think I'm older now and have grown up a lot, as I used to not like mixing with people in 'spaz chariots', as I used to call wheelchairs. Fasting today and am able to go out walking too. Freaky deaky. I think I'm a one-off, as what works for one person doesn't always work for another. That's why I learn by my mistakes. Sometimes I'm laid up, but most of the time I come through.

Thursday, 15 June 2000. Went for a swim up at the sports centre and could feel myself over doing it again, as I felt lethargic. It was going on Mondays and doing fifty minutes. I should have known better, but I hadn't overdone it for ages. I thought I'd come to a good balance of a swim for half an hour and aikido at night Tuesdays and Thursdays, but with everything else I do, it builds up. I should be taking a rest every couple of months, but I haven't been doing that lately. Aikido tonight from 8.30 to 10.00. I've got to keep my aikido up, as it gives me a buzz, and swimming is excellent for the brain. I have been doing it since Empire Pool was still in existence, hobbling up to the pool, leaving my crutches on top of the locker, and getting to the pool by holding on to walls, as I had very little balance. I have gradually built myself up from there. I bumped into Judy, who said she'd get my work published. Everything happens for a reason.

Friday, 16 June 2000. I met this boy up at Headway, Terry Evans, who suffered brain injuries, and he said he'd pick me up, so we went for an hour. It was okay, as I now am going to help people. I didn't like mixing with people in wheelchairs, but now I think I've grown up a bit. They are not born like that; they've had accidents. I used to get a lot of help, so now I'm going to give something back. I believe our lives are mapped out for us, as I always knew I'd have this accident. I think it is karma. What you did in a previous lifetime comes back to you. In my case, it wasn't what I did in a previous lifetime, it was what I did before the accident. I used to always take the piss out of people spina bifida in wheelchairs, and my nickname was Spiney, but that's another story. Now I've had this accident, and there's no way I would want to go back to what I was into before: to the demon drink, drugs, and wild women.

Saturday, 17 June 2000. I got ready for my aikido course thinking it was in Penarth. I had brekkie and got my kit ready for the course from 4.00 to 7.00. I ordered a taxi for 3.15 and got up there at 3.25, as the instructor likes practitioners to be on the mat half an hour before it starts, but there was not a soul to be seen. I had come to wrong place. Knowing there was a course, I didn't bother asking for a lift, as I usually make my own way over to Penarth and no one had offered me a lift, so I assumed it was over in Penarth. I stayed for half an hour or so, saw a few local people, and had a taxi back. Everything happens for a reason, and the reason I didn't train was that I had hurt my big toe and started to overdo it again.

Sunday, 18 June 2000. I didn't know where the course was taking place, and no one had been in touch with me. I think there is a touch of jealousy among my classmates, as I used to get picked up for courses right in the beginning to take me to places such as Swansea and Port Talbot way before courses were held at Arcot Street Church. So I phoned up Len Sinclair and went to chi kung up in Ponthir. My shoulder was fine since I rested it, but afterwards, it was giving me gyp. It must be the slow movements, so I'm back to square one again. I'll rest it again from swimming Tuesday and just go to aikido at night. I am now going to Headway up at Rookie. I wouldn't go before, as I didn't like mixing with wheelchair-bound people, thinking they had been born with mental disabilities and had not had accidents. There's a fine line between the two, but I have now come through this barrier. I had aromatherapy and reflexology at Severn Road from 1.00 to 3.00 and Japanese at Howardian High School. I was also fasting, making it my second day for last week.

Tuesday, 20 June 2000. I rested my side from swimming and aikido tonight. My swimming gives my side gyp. Since I use different muscles in aikido, I've found that I can do aikido without it giving me gyp, but I'm also having a rest from aikido. I did some t'ai chi from a video and a good amount of stretching. Len Sinclair put me off doing t'ai chi, as I've found he puts down everything that is not chi kung and that does not make him money. I've seen him taking money off people for not keeping appointments, and I don't like the way he treats people. He's does chi kung only as a moneymaking scam. There were times when I nearly didn't go, but it gave me somewhere to go, and I've got to keep on going. He only teaches you what suits him. He is a chi kung master, after all, but I've talked to a lot of people who won't go to him, as they do not like his personality.

It's all been a very slow job, but I've finally got there. The brain is a weird thing. I always knew I'd have this accident and do everything that I'm doing now to get back to health and fitness. Now I've started to go to Headway. I think I've grown up a bit, but just a bit. I don't think I'll ever really grow up. You've got to have a sense of humour or you'd just as well be dead. My improvement has been so slow, but I've kept faith in what I'm doing and know I am going to help brain-injured people up at Rookie.

I was diagnosed as being mildly euphoric shortly after the accident. March 1989 was a year to remember, as it changed my life completely for the better. I was heading six feet under the way I was carrying on with the demon drink and drugs. Most people grow out of bad habits, but it took something like this for me. It was all part of growing up. I was twenty-six when I had the accident, an age at which people usually get married or whatever. I was having such a good time that I don't think I would have grown up. I didn't start smoking cigarettes till I was seventeen, but then I got involved with the wrong company. I chose my own destiny and knew deep down that I'd come through it. But I had to go through it. I was brought up well, and my mother has been like a father and mother to the three of us. I've started doing t'ai chi from Robert Taylor's video. I'll find out where he does a class.

Wednesday, 21 June 2000. Fasting today. I had a walk down to the paper shop and over to Chapter Arts, where I studied Japanese and bought a meal for tomorrow. As I am fasting today, I just drank water, so I bought a meal for tomorrow for the entrance fee. I used to thinking about what it would be like to have an accident. Now I'm helping out at Headway up at Rookie. Some of the brain-injured people are in wheelchairs. I wouldn't go anywhere near Headway until recently, when I now realized that the people in mobile chairs have had accidents and were not born with disabilities. Now I'm helping people, as I've come through a horrific trauma with flying colours. I jokingly say that I'm top of the class, as there's nothing really wrong with me. Since the beginning I've been learning by my mistakes. Sometimes I'd be laid up, but most of the time I'd come through unscathed. So I'm doing this work and writing a book to help other people with similar injuries, but no two people are the same, and what works for one might not for the other.

Thursday, 22 June 2000. A swim up the sports centre and aikido from 8.30 to 10.00. Now everything I envisioned about having an accident and helping people up at Rookie's Headway has come true. I know it sounds far-fetched, but I knew I'd be doing this. I'd have visions of walking about very slowly and carrying papers and folders. Spooky or what?

Friday, 23 June 2000. Terry Evans picked me up at 11.30 to go to Headway. Everything I've done has pointed in the direction of helping people. I had enough help when I was a semi-cabbage.

Saturday, 24 June 2000. Today was a sporting day. I watched sports and went for a swim up at the sports centre, making it twice for the week.

Sunday, 25 June 2000. I meditated for three-quarters of an hour. I fasted today, as I fast on Sundays and Wednesdays. I've tried many combinations, but I find that fasting twice a week suits me with everything else I do.

Monday, 26 June 2000. I went to my reflexology and aromatherapy at Severn Road, but I left at 2.30, as I had a taxi coming to take me to the sports centre. The pool was open until 4.00, so I left reflexology and aromatherapy early to get my hour of swimming in. I don't go swimming the same day as aikido anymore, as the last few times it made me really tired, more than usual, as I'd been doing it for years. At home, I had tea and got ready for Japanese from 7.00 to 9.00 at the Canton Pub. I have been going to Headway at Rookie the last few Fridays because I had a lift there and back and the people are different from last time. Their brain injuries are nothing like mine. One girl's brain was like a computer that lost work; she had to relearn everything, same as me and most other people with brain injuries. She was very intelligent before the accident, whereas I'm glad about my accident. I've yet to meet anyone who is fasting twice a week and doing everything else I'm doing to prolong life. One of the helpers is involved with the Paralympics, and he's going to ask someone for a phone number for me.

Tuesday, 27 June 2000. I went for a swim at the sports centre for the second day in a row. I did my lengths for thirty-five minutes. I'm getting my fitness back up for aikido summer school. I walked home from the sports centre. I went over to the library and asked for *Writers and Artists 2000* and *The Writer's Handbook*. They had one book in, but I had to read it there, so I wrote down a few numbers. There were so many that in the end I just flicked through it and came across a number in Cardiff, Cardiff Academic Press, St Fagans Road. I went home and phoned up and told them about my accident and recovery, and the lady said they only do children's books but suggested that I write to R. G. Drake, who might be able to help. I had tea and got ready for aikido, which was from 8.00 to 10.00. When I got home from aikido, I did my Japanese from 11.00 to 11.30. I've got to do at least half an hour's practice and my meditation for three-quarters of an hour daily. I also fast twice a week religiously.

Wednesday, 28 June 2000. Fasting today plus meditation for three-quarters of an hour. I've been on the piss since January 2000. I've increased my urine intake to half a pint a day and find that amount is okay.

Thursday, 29 June 2000. I had to go to the Copthorne Hotel for a brain-awareness talk. Doctors (GPs) asked us questions to better understand the brain. Emma Langton, who is partially blind due to a brain haemorrhage, told me about this, and I got an invitation through the post. I had a lift there and back from Terry Evans, who has been taking me to Headway the last few Fridays. I then went to aikido from 8.30 to 10.00. I booked a taxi during the day to make sure I didn't dither. I had some good news about publishing my book: someone mentioned Headway doing it, and I had a word with Wendy, and she said she'd send my work off to the head office. So things are happening, and everything I've been saying all along is coming true. When I first went to Headway in Rookie it was up at the top by reception. It's all changed now. We were around a big old oblong table. I used to go when I was in hospital to get off the ward in the spaz chariot. It's all been a slow, gradual improvement, but at least I'm still improving. I've been very lucky, as everything has happened at the right time for my improvement.

Friday, 30 June 2000. I went to Headway up at Rookie, and we had swimming. Wendy said I could use their computer to put my work on a disk, as she thinks they only take disks. So I've got to take my work in to her. I'll let her read it and make the necessary adjustments, and then she'll send my work to Headway's head office. I then went home to the flat to watch the rugby league, Wigan versus Bradford, a top match between the top two in the league.

Saturday, 1 July 2000. There was rugby league on Saturday at 5.00 instead of Sunday and boxing in the evening. I've gotten into Australian rugby, as I've gotten to know the players (not personally).

Sunday, 2 July 2000. I had a reply from Mr R. G Drake, a publisher from Cardiff wishing me good luck with my book but saying it doesn't fit into his publishing system. I was fasting today and taking it easy, watching boxing, rugby league, and the European Cup final. I haven't really watched Euro 2000, but I watched the final. I haven't been sleeping much last the few days because of hot weather, which I do not like at all. My brain would much rather it be cold.

Monday, 3 July 2000. I went for a swim up at the sports centre. I stayed in the water and swam about eighteen or twenty lengths in all. I walked back. I've gone to Headway for the last four Fridays after seeing Emma Langton on a Buddhist retreat opposite Rookie. She told me about a brain awareness day up at the Copthorne Hotel. It's only the last four weeks that I've come around to mixing with people in wheelchairs. I now realize that they are normal people just like me. I had a bad accident eleven years and six months ago, in March 1989. There isn't anything wrong with me; I just walk about more slowly. I went to Disability Sport Cymru to compete in a sport. A woman gave me a pamphlet of the sports that were compatible for me together with a list of phone numbers. I fancied table tennis when I was a youngster. I still am one in my mind. You are as old as you feel, and I'll stay alive till I'm 161. I phoned Antony Munkley, who was just packing his bags to go to America, and he said to leave my address and phone number with Disability Sport Cymru and that get back to me on the 12th to give me an assessment. Had tea and got ready for Japanese from 7.00 to 9.00 in the Canton Pub, which was very handy for me, just two minutes' walk.

Tuesday, 4 July 2000. Got my swimming gear ready, cashed my money down at the post office, came back, and went for a swim. After a swim, I walked to Disability Sport Cymru, left my details with them, and walked home. I'm getting my fitness back up for summer school. It's not that I need to, but I'll feel more at ease with a hectic summer school if I do. I then got ready for aikido. My bag is always packed and ready. Lately I've been meditating for three-quarters of an hour religiously.

Wednesday, 5 July 2000. Fasting today. Took it easy with a walk down to the post office to cash money and catching up with my rugby league for the rest of the day and meditation.

Thursday, 6 July 2000. I keep meditation to three-quarters of an hour by timing myself with an alarm clock. Sometimes I'm dead on and sometimes a little over or a little under. Rob the computer whizz-kid came down at about 1.00 to do the final piece of work and print it out, as I have to take my work in to Headway for Wendy to read it and send it off to the head office. If any alterations are needed (and they probably will be), they'll do them and word it properly. I don't know if I'll have to put it all a disk or if they just want paper. Well, this is the start of something, and I'll continue to write my everyday activities, as I haven't stopped improving. I think something is going to come of the Paralympics. I'll have to wait until 12 July till Antony Munkley comes back from America.

Friday, 7 July 2000. I meditated the Buddhist way, with eyes open, as I learned when I was going to chi kung with Len Sinclair before I could see that he was only in it for the money. I went to Headway and brought my work on paper. I didn't know whether I'd have to retype it all again to save it to a disk. I'll be able to do that up at Headway House, so it's no big loss. I then had a taxi to Lula's for tea and a taxi to Penarth for aikido. I'm getting myself ready for the hectic weeks of training up at aikido summer school in Chester. Then I'll train twice a day plus a swim and a walk up to Chester Market, so I'm getting myself used to it.

At Headway I was going to go swimming but was too knackered after playing table tennis. I started off knocking the ball back and forth, and then I really got into it. I haven't played since I was fifteen, when I played for Central Boys Youth Club. It's like the bricklaying: I soon got back into it when the skill centre assessed me for work. Before I took early retirement, I did jobs in gardens (small walls and patios), but I couldn't go to a site because of the paralysis on my left side. There's really nothing wrong with me; it's just what I've been through.

Saturday, 8 July 2000. Sporty day after a busy week's training. I went out for papers and over to Chapter Arts to see what film was on tonight. Back home, I watched rugby league tapes, as only cricket, tennis, and golf were on. I had tea and went back over to Chapter Arts to watch a film. You've got to keep on the go all the time or else you'll get cheesed off, and Sunday is my complete rest day. I didn't go to chi kung, as I'm getting a bit cheesed off with it. I'm not doing any small-circuit work. It seems that Len only does what he feels like and is only training people to do the movements.

Sunday, 9 July 2000. It seems that everything is coming true. It's like something from a boy's own comic book. My intentions in life are to help people who have had accidents and brain injuries, as there was no help for me to go on. I had to learn from my mistakes right from the beginning. I've been lucky that everything has come at the right time for my improvement. Sometimes it's better to learn by your mistakes. My experience is just a guide, as what works for one person may not for another.

Monday, 10 July 2000. Went swimming over at the sports centre. We're going out for a Japanese meal tonight at 7.00 instead of having a lesson, but it will be just as good. Emma is going to Japan to work, so this is a goodbye meal and end-of-term outing.

Tuesday, 11 July 2000. I got up a bit earlier than usual, as I had a busy day. I went swimming over at the sports centre, walking there and back, and then I went to Headway to take my work, as I forgot it on Friday. I played a few games of table tennis, as Antony Munkley is going to get in touch with me on the 12th after returning from America. Table tennis is really helping my balance and co-ordination. This will be only the second time I've played, and it's really helping. I then had a taxi home, had tea, and got ready for aikido from 8.00 to 10.00 at Plasnewydd Community Hall.

Wednesday, 12 July 2000. I did my usual fast today. I went to an AGM meeting at Headway. I don't have a laptop. In fact, I have a Front Writer personal word processor.

Thursday, 13 July 2000. I'll wait till after the summer to play table tennis competitively, as it's a winter sport, and in the meantime I'll continue to play up at Headway. I can feel the improvement in balance and co-ordination. I was playing to get into the Paralympics, but it takes years of training, as I should have known from my time with Bernard Chezney. I've come around to mixing with people in wheelchairs who have had accidents, but I'm going to play up at Llanrumney Leisure Centre with able-bodied people, as there is nothing wrong with me. Had a swim up at the sports centre and then a taxi to Lula's for afternoon tea and then a taxi to Llanrumney Leisure at 7.45. I like getting there in plenty of time so I don't have to rush for an 8.30 start. I then had a taxi back at around 11.00.

Friday, 14 July 2000. I went for a swim at Headway, as it's free and I've got to see Wendy about using the computer to redo my work onto a disk that is compatible. Plus, it needs a hell of a lot of work on it before it can be sent off to be edited and made into a book. Back home at the flat, I got settled for rugby league at 7.00 for kick-off at 7.30.

Saturday, 15 July 2000. Had my usual sporty day.

Sunday, 16 July 2000. I meditated and realized I have been fasting for seven years. I don't know where the time has gone. It's eleven and a half years since the accident, and I always knew I'd be doing everything that I've been doing. Spooky, hey? Everything I've dreamt about is coming true.

Monday, 17 July 2000. Meditated for three-quarters of an hour, went swimming up at the sports centre, and tried to clean my big toe up from the infection. I had last Thursday off aikido, as I had been overdoing it and the toe was painful. I felt better for the rest. The toe was infected, so I went to the doctor's. It sounds trivial after what I've been through, but it had been giving me gyp lately. I've had the infection for ages but it's now getting worse. I cut my nail back, and it has grown back badly, so I'll have to leave it to grow back to show the doctor and have it seen to properly. I'll leave it now till after summer school. It's hereditary. The old man and my brother and sister had their nails done. I'm trying to get it to be okay for summer school up at Chester College. I then had a Japanese lesson in the Canton Pub, just two minutes' walk. I went over to Chapter Arts this afternoon to study Japanese for half an hour prior to the lesson.

Tuesday, 18 July 2000. Everything that I envisioned is coming true, almost as though I've been here before. Becoming an aikidora is such a slow job, but everyone at all grades is improving, even Kanetsuka Sensei. I had a break from swimming, as I've been overdoing things again. I only stayed in for twenty minutes yesterday, as I felt really lethargic. I had a taxi there and back to the flat. Learning Japanese is lifelong work, so there's no rush to learn. I am a slow and precise worker, and once it's in my brain, I have learned it. I'm okay on learning words, but sentences take a bit longer to sink in. I keep a book which I've written out by the side of my bed, and when I wake up in the night, I have a little read. I study for half an hour each day. *Toki-doki* (sometimes) I go over to Chapter Arts to study. From now on I'll start writing the odd *nihongo* (Japanese word) that pops in my bonce.

Wednesday, 19 July 2000. I had a nice day of rest. I fasted and rested except for a walk to cash money. I went over to Chapter Arts with my Japanese folders and bought a takeaway *gohan* (meal) for *mokuyobi* (Thursday) the 20th. I meditated for three-quarters of an hour and watched my sports.

Thursday, 20 July 2000. I was well rested after missing the last two aikido sessions after overdoing it again and my big toe giving me gyp. I watched videos. I also had a rest from swimming. I think I'll have *mokuyobi* (Thursday) aikido also. I'll try aikido tonight. My toe is giving me gyp, but it's not as bad as previously. I saw a podiatrist, and she said the toenail would have to be cut, as it's growing back rotten again. This is my life now. I cannot miss any more aikido sessions. Even though it's still painful, the brain will give off endorphins, a natural painkiller, the moment I start exercising.

Friday, 21 July 2000. At Headway I had some good news off Wendy. She was having a chat about me and my book with head office, and they discussed my doing work there, as it needs to have the grammar and spelling altered before it's sent to the head office to get published. The book will help other people who have had similar brain injuries, or maybe even the general public would find it interesting. I had nothing to go on; I learned by my mistakes. So Wendy had a word with the head office. They said not to get my hopes up, as it's virtually impossible to get a book published, but this a non-fiction book, and I think people would find it interesting. So I've got to take my portable word processor in to Headway every Friday at 11.00. I'm all right getting up if I know I'm doing something I don't mind. Adrian Mole, eat your heart out. Possibly calling the book *My Fight Back from Coma*.

Down to Lula's afterwards for tea and a haircut from my sister, Julie, and a lift home for the rugby league at 7.00 for the 7.30 kick-off.

Saturday, 22 July 2000. I went for a swim at the sports centre after having a week off. I felt lethargic in the water, so I'll have a break next week to get ready for summer school up at Chester College. My toenail is still ingrown and giving me gyp, so I'm bathing it quite often. I'll have it taken off after summer school. I'll make an appointment with Dr Lush, as you have to make the appointment two weeks in advance. Phoned Rob, and he's coming down Monday with disks and will show me how to print. Besides going on the word processor, I had a sporty day with Australian rugby league, New Zealand versus South Africa, and boxing at 8.30.

Sunday, 23 July 2000. Fasting *kyo* (today). I forgot to write in Japanese, as I was concentrating on what I was doing. I taped Australian rugby league at 8.30 and watched it later and then watched Wigan versus Hull.

Monday, 24 July 2000. I took it easy today. No swimming, as I was feeling lethargic, so I'll have the week off swimming, but I'll see how I am tomorrow about training in aikido. I'll go to aikido Thursday to sort out the lifts to Chester summer school. This might be the lull before the storm: a hectic week's training in aikido in Chester College. Got my tea sorted out and my Japanese folders and books ready for the lesson from 7.00 to 9.00 at Canton Pub, where we'll meet for maybe the last time. We've got to sort it out tonight.

Rob the computer whizz-kid came at around 6.00 to show me how to use the printer, writing it all down in sequence. At this stage in life, my activities revolve around aikido, swimming, getting my food ready, which is very important, and learning Japanese (*nihongo*).

Tuesday, 25 July (*shichigatsu*) 2000. Had a problem with my printer in the afternoon. I finally got hold of Rob at 6.00, and he sorted it out over the phone (*denwa bango*). I went to aikido from 8.00 to 10.00 at Plasnewydd Community Hall.

Wednesday, 26 July 2000. I fasted today, making it twice in a week. I took it easy with a short walk and caught up with my rugby league and boxing tapes.

Thursday (*mokuyobi*), 27 July (*shichigatsu*) 2000. Aikido from 8.30 to 10.00. I've had the last two weeks off swimming except for twenty minutes last Saturday (*dayobi*).

Friday (*kinyobi*), 28 July (*shichigatsu*). Headway at 11.00. I'm taking my portable word processor, as we are going to start working on my book in the afternoon. I got all my stuff ready for aikido summer camp up at Chester College tomorrow (*ashita*) morning for a week's training. I'll go swimming every day (*mai-nichi*).

Saturday, 29 July 2000. We set off to Chester College at 10.30. We have a day to settle in, as there are people from all over the world coming. Training actually starts tomorrow. I made the most of last week, training with a swim at 7.15 for twenty minutes, brekkie, and then getting ready for training at 9.30. I did two sessions and went for a swim at noon. I then got changed and walked to the market and got back in plenty of time for training at 2.30. I did this every day except Tuesday, when Peter Gillard advised me to watch the gradings. I filled in the night-time by going to the pictures every night except Tuesday and Friday, when I watched the rugby league. I was fine travelling up and back, even though I didn't eat till I got there. I had lift up from Gutren and back from Russel. I was totally shattered Saturday night, and Sunday I was awake at about 8.00 but dozed till about 1.30. I am so used to getting up early that it will take a few days to get back to normal.

Monday, 7 August 2000. I went for a swim at the sports centre out of habit although I was not really up to it. I felt heavy in the water but still did my ten lengths. I then had a taxi down to Lula's for tea and ended up staying the night, as I had an appointment with a podiatrist up at UWIC to see about my ingrown toenail.

Tuesday, 8 August 2000. I had a taxi to UWIC for my appointment at 11.00. They cleaned my toe and scraped it, saying it needed doing, but I couldn't do it till today. It looks 100 per cent better already. I have an appointment to get a permanent instep made, as one leg is shorter than the other due to the accident, on 5 October at 11.00. I have another appointment on 16 October at 10.15 for nail surgery. I was up at 7.15 and home by about noon. Then I had a lie down till about 2.00 and another kip after tea. I was shattered after a hectic week's training and doing everything on offer.

Wednesday, 9 August 2000. I fasted today, making it twice a week. I went for a walk to cash my money and shop for more fruit and was back about 3.00. I took it easy the rest of the day after getting myself sorted out. I watched aikido tapes till about 5.00.

My life seems to revolve around aikido, swimming, and generally sorting my life out by doing my own shopping for fruit, although I give my mother jobs to do to make her feel important. I go to Cantonian High for Japanese lessons. My Japanese teacher recommended that I do the first year over again along with the other two. One other boy is going to do the first year again too. This book is going to be a help to other people.

Thursday, 10 August 2000. I went for my swim up at the sports centre at noonish, and I gave aikido a miss tonight as I've been overdoing it again. I was on the *denwa bango* to my sister, and she said I sounded tired. I should have been resting after the hectic training last week. I've got to be careful of my toe, but I can't sit around till 16 October, when I have nail surgery.

Friday, 11 August 2000. I went for a swim up at the sports centre before going to Headway up at Rookward Hospital to do my book. Took a taxi down to Lula's for tea and then went home to watch rugby league.

Saturday, 12 August 2000. Sporty weekend. I can't get my sleeping pattern back to normal. Since summer school I've been waking early, around 6.00. I try reading, but that doesn't always work. I got used to swimming twice a day. I finally got my chequebooks from Mr Hibbit, as my money is being transferred to my name. I've got to re-invest. But to save all the hassle, I've spoken to Mr Simmons, the investor for the Court of Protection, and I'm going to keep the investments and pay them privately. I'm just waiting for a card, as I have got the paying-in book and chequebook. It's all been a very slow job, but I think I am now capable of handling my own money and affairs with a lot of help, mainly from my mother. I believe that I'm destined to have my own club for aikido with a built-in swimming pool and for people with disabilities and those who are able-bodied. When I had the accident, I had nothing and no one to follow, so I'm writing this book to help people who have had accidents. I class myself as normal. I've had an accident, but there is nothing wrong with me, I just get around more slowly. I imagine an awful lot of brain-injured people feel the same way. Today I went down the rugby union, Cardiff versus Leicester. Cardiff were convincing winners. I then went down Lula's and had a lift home from my sister. I did what I had to do and settled down for boxing at 8.00.

Sunday, 13 August 2000. I fasted today, listened to music, and watched footie, Man United versus Chelsea in the Charity Cup. I'm writing up the last few days' events on my computer.

Monday, 14 August 2000. I had a taxi to Lula's as I was feeling as though I needed a rest from swimming. I watched a few aikido videos and was feeling progressively rougher as the day went on. I was going to my Japanese lesson in the Canton Pub not knowing if it was this week or next week, and alas, it was next week. So I went home to the flat, got my swimming kit together, and phoned for a taxi to the sports centre for swimming from 7.00 to 9.00. I felt much better after a swim. As I've said, it's a good therapy for the brain. After Chester I thought I needed a rest and didn't go at my usual time to get my swim out of the way, but I realize how important swimming is to me.

Tuesday, 15 August 2000. I went for a swim at the sports centre, which did me good as usual, and had aikido from 8.00 to 10.00 at Plasnewydd Community Hall. As soon as I get a sweat on, it gives me a buzz. At present I swim and do aikido. With living on my own and sorting out my food and other necessities, I find it's enough. I'm also learning Japanese, and I'm going to enrol in a vegetarian cookery course at Cardiff High.

Wednesday, 16 August 2000. Today was my fasting day. I'm going to put my fasting back to three times a week starting Friday. I cashed my money, popped in the health shop for chamomile tea, and went over to Chapter Arts, where I did my Japanese. I then went over to the Principality and finally over to Tesco to stock up on my fruit and to get fags for Lula. I object to people smoking and stay right away, as it could lead to cancer, but people who know me don't smoke in front of me, and I don't mind Lula smoking, as having a nice fag is all she looks forward to. I also wrote down a number for Wild Goose Chi Kung. Sessions are £25 and from 2.00 6.00 on 3 September, and classes start on 14 September and go from 6.00 to 7.00. So I'll go to aikido afterwards, if it all goes well when I phone.

Thursday, 15 August 2000. I went swimming at the sports centre and did aikido from 8.30 to 10.00. I fit my *gohans* (meals) around my training. Between swimming and aikido, I went over to the Chapter Arts, where I studied my Japanese and did some writing. I went home for my tea and was ready for the taxi to aikido at 7.45.

Friday, 16 August 2000. A big day today. Had a taxi to Headway, as I had to see if the disk from Rob the computer boffin would be compatible with the computer at Headway. It was, so that was a weight off my mind. I knew all along it would be all right, as Rob said all my work is on there and that I shouldn't get rid of it just because it doesn't work on my word processor. The computer at Headway corrects all your spelling and re-edits your work for you. That's how far technology has progressed. I had a taxi down to Lula's and a taxi home to the flat. Boxing preview at 7.00 and rugby league at 7.30.

Saturday, 17 August 2000. My body clock hasn't been the same since going away to aikido summer school. I was up at about 9.00, had a taxi to the market, and saw a few people. I walked down Lula's, watched my rugby league, had tea, and went home about 7.00. I watched the boxing tonight, a pay-to-view event, and was up till 4.45 a.m. So I was very tired the next day. I awoke at about 10.00 and taped the Australian rugby league play-offs. I didn't go back to sleep, but I was overtired and just stayed in bed with my music on, getting up only to change CDs.

Monday, 21 August 2000. I awoke at about 10.00 and got up, as I had a full day. Every day is a full day, but today was full without training except a swim. I went over to Tesco for my fruit before having a taxi to the sports centre for a swim. The I had a taxi to Lula's, where I watched my rugby league and aikido tapes before having tea and taking a taxi to my Japanese lesson at the Canton Pub from 7.00 to 9.00.

Tuesday, 22 August 2000. Awake at 9.30 but didn't have a good night's sleep, so I wasn't up until 10.30. Brekkied, shat, showered, and shaved, my ablutions. Went for a swim up at the sports centre. I swim three times a week, Monday, Tuesday, and Thursday. I plan my week around my aikido, which I do twice a week, and Wednesday and Sunday are my fasting days. Wednesday I cash my money, and *nichiyobi* (Sunday) is complete rest, with only a short walk to the bin. Had my tea, which is a very important part of my routine. You've got to eat to live, not live to eat. I did my Feldenkrais exercises, which I haven't done for a few months because of minor injuries. I had a nap after tea and got ready to go to aikido.

Wednesday, 23 August 2000. I was fasting today. I try to stay in bed till noon and having a number of reads. Went for a walk down to the post office, the health shop, and to Chapter Arts, where I learned my Japanese from the folder I carried in my bag. I also went to the library, the Principality, and over to Tesco for more fruit. I like to keep ahead. I got home and organized my fruit and putzed around till I watched a rugby league match on tape and footie at 8.00.

Thursday, 24 August 2000. Had a rough sleep but was still up at 10.30, brekkied, shat, showered, and shaved, and went swimming at 12.30. I'm back up to my half an hour's swim. I do front crawl, backstroke, and breaststroke and a bit of stretching. I decided when I got up to give aikido a miss today, as could feel myself overdoing it again. I've stopped myself this time, but I still tend to overdo it.

Friday, 25 August 2000. Felt better after I rested from aikido last night. I went to Headway to work on my book over in the computer room. There is no need to take my word processor, as Rob's disc was not compatible with mine, but it works over on the computer. It's going to be a slow and tedious job, but there's no rush. It's being sent to Headway head office after being doctored, so to speak, three times. Down to Lula's after Headway at 4.00 for tea and home to the flat at 6.30 for rugby league.

Saturday, 26 August 2000. I'm going down to the rugby union today. I had a taxi to town to the market. I went to a record stall and a bookstall to see Colin, with whom I'm going down to the rugby union to see Cardiff versus Neath. I went down to Lula's for tea and back home to watch boxing and footie. I phoned up for an appointment to do Pilates. I didn't really know what it was about and asked the man there to explain. It seems a good therapy, and I asked him to work on my hips and lower back.

Sunday, 27 August 2000. I awoke at 9.30 and got up at 10.30. I'm learning to listen to my body, so I decided to eat. Big sporting weekend with Rugby league and the Australian Rugby League grand final from 1.00 to 3.00 and had a lie down. Whilst making tea, I ended up watching *Front Row*, a programme about rugby union. I taped the second half of the footie and finally watched Wigan versus Bradford at 6.30, a cracking match right down to the last kick, with Wigan winning 20-19.

Monday, 28 August 2000. I decided to eat today. I went to Japanese (*nihongo*) over at the Canton Pub not knowing if anyone would turn up or if I'd got it wrong, but I couldn't remember anyone mentioning a bank holiday today. Went down to Lula's with a few aikido videos and started the week off by taking it easy today. No swimming. I'll go back to swimming twice a week, which fits in well with my other activities, which include aikido twice a week and swimming on as well on Tuesday. I have Japanese classes on Monday and Wednesday, a day of rest, and Headway on Friday. I've been overdoing things the last few months by swimming three times a week, but now I'll go back to twice a week.

Tuesday, 29 August 2000. I made an appointment with Capel Cure's Cardiff branch with Andy Stansfield at 1.00 at his office in town at 29 Windsor Place, as I'm taking over my own investments. I'm taking Mother along for support and to ensure that I'm not an easy touch for investors. Went swimming at the sports centre. The temperature has dropped, which suits me fine, as I don't like hot weather since the accident. I can go back to swimming twice a and really go for it non-stop for thirty-five minutes, which works out well for my other activities also. Had a taxi there and back, had tea and a lie down for three-quarters of an hour whilst playing a CD. Got up refreshed and did some writing on my word processor. Then I did some Feldenkrais exercises and played an aikido video whilst waiting for a taxi, which I ordered for 7.45 for the 8.00 start of aikido at Plasnewydd Community Hall.

Wednesday, 30 August 2000. Today was my fasting day. I ate Sunday, as I listened to my body. I took a short walk to cash money and took it easy the rest of the day. I went over to the Chapter Arts, where I studied my Japanese for half an hour. I stick to my regimen. I watched rugby league tapes, read the papers, and did the business I had to do.

Thursday, 31 August 2000. I had an appointment with Andy Stansfield from Capel Cure Investments. The meeting went well.

I was glad it was all settled. It's a worry off my mind, although a nice worry. I walked to town to the record shop and bought a few CDs in MVC and walked to the market to see a few people and then back to flat for tea and a lie down. I had a rest from aikido, as I did a lot of walking and mind work, but I'm going on an aikido course with Kanetsuka Sensei on *dayobi* (Saturday) from 5.00 to 7.00. I've got to make sure I train twice a week, as it's such a slow job that any more is pointless. It's a lifelong martial art; everything is done very slowly and precisely. There are no shortcuts. It's not like karate or judo, where you become black belt in two or three years. No one's in any rush. I treat this as advanced physiotherapy, as it's for the brain and is also a self-defence discipline. I'll go swimming tomorrow after Headway. I'll go back to twice a week, as I find swimming a very important therapy.

Friday, 1 September 2000. I feel well rested after giving aikido a miss yesterday. I had to work on my book at Headway, and this week the computers were free at 10.30, so I had to get up early. I had a taxi at about 10.00 to Headway at Rookie. I don't mind getting up if I know I've got somewhere to go and things to do. I had some good news: Maureen, who is teaching computers, is going to edit my work for me, for a fee, of course. Doing it myself would take years. I then went for a swim up at the sports centre and took a taxi to Lula's. I had a lie down listening to music and then took a taxi home to the flat at 6.30 for rugby league. In all I had five taxis. Fiona from my Japanese lesson says it's good to listen to Japanese tapes. I thought I had two tapes, but the first one is blank. I've had them nearly a year now and I've still not listened to them.

Saturday, 2 September 2000. I was supposed to go on an aikido course, as I stated Thursday, but I've got a chi kung seminar Sunday with Keith from 2.00 to 6.00, plus mini courses from 6.00 to 7.00 on Thursdays. I fasted today, making it twice this week. Aikido is a lifelong art, so training twice a week is fine, even though I missed it Thursday because I needed the rest. I had a taxi to MVC in town, where I bought a few CDs. Then I walked to Cardiff Arms Park and watched Cardiff beat Edinburgh Reivers by 80 points to 16. I then walked to Lula's. I did all this whilst fasting, but I've done it before, so I knew how to handle it and was okay. After a taxi back home to the flat, I bathed, watched Bridgend versus Llanelli on the Welsh and footie at 7.30, England versus France.

Sunday, 3 September 2000. Everything is happening at the right time for my improvement, as I've said before. It's been a very slow job, but it's not something you rush. I had some more good news Friday. Maureen, the computer teacher up at Headway, mentioned a computer course up at the Friary. I've already been to that and don't want to learn computers. I only want to work on my book, but Maureen said it doesn't work like that. She said I have to learn computers. We got talking, and Maureen is going to do work for me privately with a view to getting my book published. Without her help, it would take me another five years or more to complete it. I don't want to learn computers. Up at the Friary before, I didn't get on with computers. I also went over to Chapter Arts for a chi kung seminar from 2.00 to 6.00. It went fine.

Monday, 4 September 2000. I awoke at 8.00, had *nomimasu* (a drink), and read but didn't go back to sleep, as I had things on my mind. I had to exchange the CDs I bought. I bought them on the guy behind the bar's recommendation, in a bit of a rush. I had brekkie, etc., and took a taxi to the sports centre for a swim, a taxi to MVC and exchanged the CDs with no problem, and a taxi to Lula's. I had a lie down and listened to music at teatime and took a taxi to my Japanese lesson at the Canton Pub. It was an excellent lesson, as only the sensei (teacher) and I were there. The other two students never turned up. The sensei asked if I'd like to go over what we'd already done, and I was all for it, so we revised, and she said I did fine.

Tuesday, 5 September 2000. I now swim three times a week, Monday, Tuesday, and Thursday, for thirty or thirty-five minutes with some stretching up at the sports centre. I do aikido from 8.00 to 10.00. Coming up to winter, I tend to get up early. I'm usually up at about 8.00, and I go to bed at about 11.00. I go straight to sleep. Through the summer, I tended to wake at 8.00, have a read, and go back to sleep.

Wednesday, 6 September 2000. I did my usual fast today and had a dentist appointment at 12.30 at another private practice at the Parade, as Wyn Jenkins was overcharging me. I went for a check-up with the new dentist, which cost £65. I had my doubts about Wyn Jenkins from the beginning, and his prices have shot up since the last time I saw him, so I know he was taking me for a ride.

Wednesday, 6 September 2000. I was fasting today. I had a taxi to the new private dentist, as the other dentist was taking my money for things I didn't need done. Afterwards I took a taxi to Lula's to clear my videos. Mother was up at Julie's, so I didn't see much of her, as I went at 7.00 to watch live footie and tape the rugby union at 7.30. Things are starting to happen since I've had my chequebook. I've paid for dental work, a Pilates course and Wild Goose Chi Kung, enrolled in a Japanese course for the year, and am going on a kum nye retreat at Lam Rim Buddhist Centre at Raglan on the 8th, 9th, and 10th.

Thursday, 7 September 2000. Went for a swim at the sports centre around noon and gave aikido a miss, as I have a kum nye retreat coming up. Lula came down, and I let her pack my bag with my supervision. I find her jobs to do, as she is on her own. The kum nye retreat starts Friday afternoon and finishes Monday. It's some sort of healing, so this might be what I've been looking for. I have tried many healing activities. Everyone is a healer, you just need to channel your energy the correct way. I had a taxi to Newport Station, as I had bags to carry, and from there I took a bus from Newport to Raglan. I phoned Margaret when I arrived at Raglan at 5.28 to come and pick me up and take me to Lam Rim Buddhist Centre.

Chapter 7

I have lost about four weeks of my work since I gave the disks and the work that Rob had printed out for me to Headway. My routine now goes like this: Monday I go swimming up at the sports centre in the afternoon, get my munchies (tea) ready, and have a lie down after tea to recharge my batteries. Then I'm ready for my Japanese class at Cantonian High. Jane advised me to do the first year of Japanese again, but I had already decided to anyway. For the first six months of the course, I went to get out. It was only in the second six months that I studied properly (*ubenkiyoed*).

Tuesday, 26 September 2000. I get up early, as I like this weather. The heat is no good for me. I went swimming up at the sports centre, sorted out my grub, had a lie down whilst listening to music so I just dozed, and then I was off to Pilates with John Bruno over in Penarth. I then went to aikido from 8.00 to 10.00. On average, I take four or five taxis a day.

Wednesday, 27 September 2000. I fasted, watched aikido tapes, listened to music, and had a short walk to get papers. I now have Japanese lessons twice a week. Today Jane, the teacher, Ffione, and Dave came around to my flat. We are going to alternate who hosts the lesson. Next week, we'll go to Ffione's flat.

Thursday, 28 September 2000. I went to UWIST by taxi and then had another taxi to the sports centre for a swim. Then I went home for tea and a lie down, and I was off to Chapter Arts across the road for chi kung for an hour and then back to the flat. I phoned a taxi to take me to aikido in Llanrumney. I'm feeling totally knackered, but no pain, no gain, as they say. The chi kung I'm doing is called 'Wild Goose'. It's purely for health and there are no martial-arts movements. I've been to another dentist, Mr Guppy, at the Parade opposite Wyn Jenkins, who was ripping me off. I've also been to see Cardiff Rugby play at the Millennium.

Friday, 29 September 2000. I was up 8.30, as I had to go to Headway at Rookie. It went very well. I'm slowly coming around to mixing with the people there. I found out that most of the people there have had a brain injury of some sort. I had a good chat with Wendy the organizer. I said I was thinking of starting my own centre with a health and fitness club that offered aikido. She said, 'Well, what do you think this is then?'

Saturday, 30 September 2000. I tore a muscle in my back a few weeks ago, and now I realize that the only way to heal it is with complete rest, but it is very hard to do nothing at all. I've learned to rest on weekends, but now I have to have a complete rest and not carry anything at all, as I've been aggravating it by training in aikido, swimming, and carrying things. Flump (my brother) and Stevie came around to fix the bathroom lock. A sporty day today with Olympics and boxing in the evening.

Sunday, 1 October 2000. I have been fasting for seven years and two months, give or take a few weeks. I had my usual sporty Sunday with music and television. I also have neglected to say that I type my training routine on my word processor at least four times a week.

Monday, 2 October 2000. My back muscles are still giving me gyp. I've had the problem for a few weeks, but I keep aggravating it by training, swimming, and carrying things. The pain is my brain's way of saying that my body needs to rest, but I always leave it till I'm unfit to do anything. I went down Lula's in the afternoon and had a taxi to my Japanese class from 7.00 to 9.00 at Cantonian in Fairwater.

Tuesday, 3 October 2000. I had a well-deserved rest from aikido and swimming. I just went to Pilates with John Bruno, as I have paid for five lessons. I have been doing everything I can to make myself soft and supple, as a taught, rigid body will give you problems in later life. I have been drawn to things at the right time for my improvement. It all started with the accident. Afterwards I was lucky that my brain went the right way and enabled me to train my body and mind back to get back to health and fitness. My brain could have gone the other way, and I could have plonked myself in front of the television, if I made it that far. I do a lot more than most people, as there's nothing really wrong with me; I've just been through a lot. I eventually got myself fit enough to hobble up to the Empire Pool, leave my crutches on top of a locker and get to the pool by holding on to the walls.

In the pool, I started off doing widths to get my strength and fitness back up. I also used to phone a taxi to take me to Channel View Leisure Centre, where I lifted light weights. I used to go to Ray Wounacott's karate class and do the exercises in the front of the class. I was then spotted by Ray's mate from the Army, Glyn Grey, who ran a course for people with special needs, and I trained there for a while. Eventually I saw an advertisement for aikido and hobbled along there. I didn't use crutches then, but I still had a walking stick for long distances. I remember saying to Sensei Peter Gillard that I'd had a bad accident in March 1989 but that there was nothing really wrong; I just had trouble with my balance. I started training in aikido and improved enormously. I used to go to all of Kanetsuka's courses. In Severn Road, I did t'ai chi, computers, and, by 1997, chi kung with Len Sinclair. Now I do chi kung at Chapter Arts across the road and Pilates in Penarth with John Bruno. I also attend Lam Rim Buddhist Centre at Raglan, where I've found another therapy that makes me soft and supple, kum nye with John Peacock. I knew nothing about it, but I was drawn to it like I have been to everything else I've done.

Wednesday, 4 October 2000. I had yet another busy day today. I had a shiatsu appointment at 11.00. This was a softer treatment than previous shiatsu treatments I've had. I then went to the flat and had something to eat, as I had a busy day planned. Food is very important, especially in winter. Then I had a dental appointment. I saw the hygienist at 1.40 and the dentist at 2.40. I took a taxi home to the flat, where I had tea and a lie down for half an hour. Then I was off to a Japanese lesson at Ffione's house. My back muscles were playing me up a bit, but all you can do for something like that is rest.

Thursday, 5 October 2000. I went for a short swim on my back with the float Tuesday. I did eight lengths and was fine, so I went again today. After four lengths, I decided to have a swim. I did six lengths and came out unscathed. I could feel it later, though, so I went ahead with my plan of no aikido and took it easy, as rest and relaxation is just as important as exercise, especially when you've got to rest. I phoned the podiatry unit at Western Avenue to cancel my appointment to have a permanent instep made, which costs £45. I had a talk with the boss, and he said that the one I've got will last for a long time and the permanent ones last only three or four years, so I'll wait till the one I have goes. I've still got an appointment on 16 October 2000 for nail surgery. I gave my chi kung from 6.00 to 7.00 a miss tonight, as slow movement hinders the back, as I found out with Len Sinclair. Besides, I'm healthy enough without it. I am going to live for 161 years. I know this because I used to have dreams just after the accident that would come true. I used to dream of horses, and they'd win at good odds, and it's been proven that people with brain injuries are partly psychic.

Friday, 6 October 2000. I went to Headway and gave my disk to Tony, who is going to add a brief account of my accident and the improvements that I've made. I then went for a swim up at the sports centre. My back was still giving me gyp, but a swim eased it. I always thought of the back as only the lower back. I didn't realize that it was all the muscles in the back of the torso and the shoulders. The physios at Rookie said I might suffer from back problems, but I didn't realize the pain was in the muscles as well, and I've had problems with the muscles in my back for years. I went down to Lula's after a swim and then went home to watch rugby union, as rugby league is on tomorrow.

Saturday, 7 October 2000. I woke at 8.30, as my sleeping patterns have changed with the weather. I had a taxi to town, where I went to the market, to MVC for CDs. Then I walked down Lula's, where I watched Newport versus Munster Union and had tea. Then I got home for the 5.30 kick-off of rugby league and then watched boxing and a film.

Sunday, 8 October 2000. Fasting today. I took it easy and decided not to do chi kung. The brain needs a rest. It's only when something happens, like I injure my back muscles, that I rest. I've got nail surgery Monday, 16 October 2000, so I'll be off aikido for and swimming for three weeks. I started resting up a few weeks ago. I've been swimming and aggravated my back, but it's difficult to do nothing.

Monday, 9 October 2000. I'm having a rest from swimming. I had a dental appointment at 2.00 at the Parade, had a taxi down to Lula's, and had another taxi to Japanese at Cantonian High School, and had a taxi home.

Tuesday, 10 October 2000. I walked down the road to cash money. My back is very slowly improving. I had a bath with juniper and ginger and lay in the bath instead of going in and out as usual. The back is a very complex thing. I thought the problem was with the lower back and that I would be fine if I went for a swim, but I didn't realize that the problem was with all the muscles also. I now understand that the only way to cure the injury is to have complete rest, but that's easier said than done. I stayed in and went on the computer and was up and down all afternoon with a lot of pain. I decided to go to Pilates to exercise the abdominal area over in Penarth, as I already paid. I'll sort out when I'll go again. I study my Japanese every day and have just bought a Japanese textbook for my private lesson on Wednesday. Come 3.00 p.m., I was fed up, so I decided to go swimming, and it did my back muscles good. Any sort of training gives me a buzz because the brain gives off its own natural painkiller. I then did Pilates from 6.00 to 7.00 and had a lot of discomfort. At the end of the class, I asked the instructor if there were any courses he could recommend, and he gave me the name of Ian Newton and his phone number.

Wednesday, 11 October 2000. I was fasting today and went out for a walk to cash my money. I've got into a routine of not eating Wednesday and Sunday. I nearly didn't eat Tuesday, but that would have put me all out. I phoned Ian Newton and explained that John Bruno gave me his number and that I would like to take John Bruno's training further. Ian Newton was out, but his assistant said that there's a practitioners' course starting 20 October and that she'd send me details. I'll ask John Bruno what he advises. My dream of having my own club is coming true. It's still early days, but I think my club will offer aikido, health and fitness activities, and a section for people like myself who've had accidents and suffered brain injuries. There is nothing really wrong with me, I just get about more slowly, but everyone is different, and what's right for one will not be right for another. My Japanese comrades Jane Kajemoto, Ffione, and Criss, are coming around tonight. I am repeating the first year again on Mondays on Jane's advice and have private lessons on Wednesdays.

Thursday, 12 October 2000. My back was still giving me gyp, but I worked through the pain and went to aikido, as I'll be off for three or four weeks after my nail surgery next Monday, and it seems ages since I last went. I have to get the nail surgery done, as it grows back all the time. I also went swimming.

Friday, 13 October 2000. I went to Headway up at Rookie, where we went for a swim. I'm now on the Internet. From being in a wheelchair to swimming to living on my own to doing aikido and, since fourteen months ago, to learning Japanese, I've improved a lot. I stayed down at Lula's and went home Saturday afternoon for the super league grand final, Wigan versus St Helens. I also watched two European rugby union matches. Rugby union is much more exiting now that they've got this final competition. Before they were just going through the motions week in and week out in the Welsh league, and all teams new the others' games inside out.

Sunday, 14 October 2000. I fasted today and took it easy. I had another sporty day watching rugby and then had nail surgery up at UWIST. I'll stay down Lula's for a few days, as I don't really know how bad the recovery will be. I'll probably have to keep my foot up to allow it to heal, but that's easier said than done, as you know by now I can't keep still for long. I'll have to keep still with this or it will never heal.

Tuesday, 17 October 2000. I've got to keep my foot up, as otherwise it will take longer to heal, but I think I've now learned by my mistakes. I went to UWIST to have the bandage changed and made another appointment for a week's time to have a check-up. I'm down at Lula's so that I won't do anything. Well, so I'll do as little as possible. My back is fine as long as I'm careful and wary of carrying things, as that was the mistake I made before.

Wednesday, 18 October 2000. I had a Feldenkrais appointment at 2.00 with Darien Pritchard. I explained that I'd had my toe chopped, and he said he'd loosen me up on the couch. My body has been told to rest. The brain is telling me to slow down.

Thursday, 19 October 2000. I went and watched aikido, and it still did me good as I picked up some things. It's surprising what you pick up by just watching. I also gave my website details to about six people.

Friday, 20 October 2000. I went to Headway, and Tony, who put up my website, got into the site, but it didn't show the full story. Only Tony knows what he did.

Saturday, 21 October 2000. I had a sporty weekend watching Cardiff RFC beat Saracens in the European Cup on telly down at Lula's. I also had a small bet for a bit of interest.

Sunday, 22 October 2000. I fasted today and had another small bet.

Monday, 23 October 2000. It's my second week off after having my toe chopped, and I've just been taking it easy, but I'm itching to get back to normal activities. They said up at UWIST that I'd be off for three or four weeks, but everyone is different. I might be off aikido longer; I'll stay off till it's completely healed.

Tuesday, 24 October 2000. I did my shopping as usual to stock up and had an appointment at 3.00 at UWIST to check on my toe. It's fine; I just have to keep doing what I've been doing and have another appointment in two weeks. I asked about swimming and aikido, and the doctor said not to do those till the toe is healed right over to prevent infection. I've done everything they've said, as I don't want to go back too soon, as that will put me back ages. I went and watched aikido from 8.00 to 10.00 at Plasnewydd Community Hall. It's better to keep to my schedule of nights out, as otherwise I'd get right pissed off. I've stopped drinking my own urine, and I feel much better for it. I was getting slight injury problems, and those were the brain's way of letting me know it was not good for me. I did it for ten months, but now I'm off the piss.

Wednesday, 25 October 2000. I ate today, as I had a Feldenkrais appointment at 2.00. The practitioner gets me on the table and loosens me up. I had Japanese from 7.00 to 9.00 at my flat. Ffione and I alternate weeks.

Thursday, 26 October 2000. I went and put £200 in my savings account. That leaves me £3,200 after drawing my money out from the Principality. I can spend the interest every year, and as long as I leave a fiver in, the bank won't close the account. I fasted today and also went to watch aikido Llanrumney Leisure Centre.

Friday, 27 October 2000. I went to Headway to see about the Internet. My article has not come out, and only Tony knows the procedure. I took a taxi to Lula's and went to see Cardiff versus Saracens in a big European Cup match. Cardiff has already won away.

Saturday, 28 October 2000. I had a taxi down to Lula's and watched the rugby league World Cup all afternoon. Then I had tea and a taxi home, watched more rugby league at 6.30 and boxing from 8.30 to 10.00, and to round off a sporty day, I watched the footie.

Sunday, 29 October 2000. More rugby league in the afternoon and Wales versus Cook Islands at 6.30. Of course, I fasted.

Monday, 30 October 2000. It was two weeks ago that I had my toe cut, and it's healed nicely. I think I can go swimming tomorrow, as I have a busy day today. I have to see Caroline at Severn Road for peppermint, go to the dentist at 2.30 for two and a half hours, take a taxi to Lula's, and take another taxi at 6.30 to Cantonian High for Japanese.

Tuesday, 31 October 2000. I stayed home for the toe and watched aikido videos. Lula did my shopping for me so I could rest my toe and my shoulder. Next day I fasted and went to Feldenkrais, having asked Darien Pritchard last week if it would be all right not to eat.

Thursday, 2 November 2000. I went to UWIST for a check-up on my toe, and the doctor said it was healing nicely but that I shouldn't do nothing till there's no pus visible on the dressing when I get up in morning. I have another appointment for December 12, so I won't do anything till then, as activity would only put me back. My Japanese videos came today. I now only go to the lesson on a Monday. I stopped going privately, as I felt I was getting ripped off.

Friday, 3 November 2000. I went to Headway and gave Tony my disk so he can add to the story about my training since the accident. I went down to Lula's for tea and had a quiet night in, as no sport was on.

Saturday, 4 November and Sunday, 5 November. I went to the Natural Health Show up at the students' union. I've been going for years now, and they hold the show twice a year. I had prebooked for two talks about healing. The talk on Sunday was with Jack Temple, and I think I'll take it further. I bought electromagnetic insoles from one of the stalls and went to a few talks about nutrition. I'm doing everything right, but I just wanted to be told that. I've got an appointment on naturopathic nutrition Monday, 12 November.

Tuesday, 7 November 2000. I went to the dentist at 2.30 for the final time to have caps fitted, and then I went to watch aikido from 8.00 to 10.00 at Plasnewydd Community Hall. I've to go back to UWIST on 12 December and will not go swimming till my toe is healed completely and even longer before practicing aikido.

Wednesday, 8 November 2000. I had a Feldenkrais appointment at 2.00. The practitioner says I've improved a lot since I first came about eighteen months ago. I'm feeling my way around things now where I'd lose my balance before. I then went down to Lula's for tea and went home to my flat about 6.00. I ate today as I did a late fast on Monday. I'll fast again tomorrow.

Thursday, 9 November 2000. I fasted today, as I ate yesterday, and I went to watch aikido at Llanrumney Leisure Centre. It was a bit of a pain to watch, but I've got to or else I'll be off for longer after my toe heals. A lot of my old injuries have healed whilst I've been off.

Friday, 10 November 2000. I went to Headway, where I saw about my book and saw Tony about the articles I've done on the Internet. I also saw Maureen, and we agreed to sort out money and other details for her work on my book in two weeks, as she's off till then. I then went down to Lula's, and Stephen (my brother-in-law) and took the kids to the Millennium Stadium to watch Wales A versus New Zealand A. There were a lot of families and loads of kids there.

Saturday, 11 November 2000. I had a ticket for Wales versus Samoa at 4.00. It was a great match, with Wales winning. The night before, Wales were winning 9-3 with ten minutes to go, but New Zealand scored three quick tries and converted them.

Sunday, 12 November 2000. I fasted today and took it easy by watching Lennox Lewis versus David Tua, which I taped last night because I went to bed at 1.30.

Sunday, 12 November 2000. I did my twice-weekly fast and took it easy, listening to music and watching Wales rugby league progress to the semi-finals of the World Cup. Wales are playing Australia, but I'll always stick by Wales no matter who they are playing. I think I'll have a small bet on them to beat Australia at long odds.

Monday, 13 November 2000. It's been five weeks since my nail surgery, but I can't go swimming (in case of infection) until 12 December, and I can't do aikido for even longer. I don't think I'll go back before Christmas. Twice my toe has looked good and I have said to myself, 'I'm going to go swimming tomorrow,' but when I got up the next day, a scab had formed. I think that's the body's way of telling me to rest. I had an appointment with the nutritionist scheduled, but I cancelled, as I'm healthy enough as it is without someone telling me what I already know.

Tuesday, 14 November 2000. I went down to cash my money at the post office and went to Chapter Arts to study (*yubinokio*) Japanese. It takes me two hours to do my ablutions, my SSS and bath, in the morning after brekkie. Through the winter I'm in bed by midnight and up at about 10.00 although I'm awake at about 8.00. I read in bed but do not go back off except in the summer and spring, when I need to stay out of the sun. My schedule in the summer is the brain's way of telling me to stay out of the sun. I have seen a programme about the brain that said it prefers cold. I went and watched aikido at Plasnewydd Community Hall from 8.00 to 10.00 to stay in my routine. I've got to stay off swimming till 12 December, when I go back to UWIST for my check-up. I'll be off aikido even longer.

Wednesday, 15 November 2000. I had a Feldenkrais appointment at 2.00 to loosen me up whilst I'm inactive. The practitioner is giving me exercises to improve my mobility and to help me walk as normally as possible. The movements are very intricate, as everything is connected. Today he did my feet for balance, having me put my weight to the left, to the centre, and to the right. There are only five or six trained Feldenkrais practitioners in Great Britain, so I was very lucky to find Darien Pritchard. A few times when I've thought about swimming, I've got up the next day to find my toe scabbed up, so I stay off it and have a good rest and do other things to keep busy.

Thursday, 16 November 2000. I fasted today, as I ate yesterday. I've got to fast twice week, usually Sunday and Wednesday, but I've altered my routine whilst I'm off swimming and aikido. An injury is the body's way of telling me to slow down. I went over to Chapter Arts to study Japanese for an hour, and then I went home to the flat and putzed about for a few hours, as I can't keep still, and then I ordered a taxi to take me to Llanrumney Leisure Centre to watch aikido. I pick up quite a lot listening to Peter Gillard talk.

Friday, 17 November 2000. There were no free computers up at Headway, so I gave that a miss, as I don't like the smoking. I went for the afternoon down to Lula's to watch rugby league tapes. I returned home at around 7.00 and settled down for an evening's viewing.

Saturday, 18 November 2000. I put ads up for a proofreader to hedge my bets, so to speak, so I'll know *ikura deska*, how much the book's going to cost. I put one up over in Chapter Arts and another in the health shop. I then took a taxi down to Lula's and stayed until about 6.00. I had a letter from Sharpham College for Buddhist Studies, which John Peacock referred me to after the course up at Lam Rim Buddhist Centre.

Saturday, 18 November 2000. It was a big weekend for rugby, both union and league. Wales just got beaten by Australia in league, and Wales beat America in union.

Monday, 19 November 2000. I walked up and down Canton looking to have my book seen to. I finally got a name and a *denwa bango*, a phone number, from the library receptionist. I phoned up and spoke to Angela Cutler. We had a good chat, and I have an appointment at 11.00 next Monday, the 27th. I had a taxi down to Lula's and a taxi to Japanese. I gave Jane Kajemoto my pamphlet to translate from my Japanese video. She says my Japanese has improved, which is good to hear. I seem to improve in everything I do, which is excellent. I was all set to go swimming again, but my toe leaked pus again, so I phoned up UWIST to tell them what happened, and they suggested I come in at 2.00.

Wednesday, 22 November 2000. Walked down to cash my cheque and took my Japanese books with me to chapter arts to study (*ubinkokyio*) for half an hour. I then went home to the flat and phoned Margaret at Lam Rim Buddhist Centre to get the times of buses from Newport to Raglan. I'll get a taxi to Newport to get there in plenty of time to catch the bus at 4.10. I'm going for yet another weekend course. I stayed down at Lula's, as I went to Millennium Stadium, where Wales lost to South Africa. I arrived home at 1.00. I fasted today, but I went out at 8.00 to watch aikido. The last couple of months I've been betting, but I'll give it up again, as it was starting to get hold of me. I started to bet over the phone on who was the best player in the rugby league. I usually bet on Keiron Cunningham, but this time I changed, and you guessed, Cunningham won, so gambling is out.

Friday, 24 November 2000. I went to Headway to see how much (*ikura desuka*) the work on my book would cost me. I'll suggest that Maureen and I get together once or twice a week for an hour or two, as she has only a couple of hours to spare a week. I then went to Lam Rim Buddhist Centre for a samatha meditation retreat with Rupert Gethin. I had a taxi to Newport to get there in plenty of time to catch the bus to Raglan at 4.10. The schedule at the Buddhist centre gives participants a full day. I arrived at about 5.30, in plenty of time to unpack and get my things sorted before supper at 6.30. From 7.30 to 8.20 I did the praises and requests to the twenty-one taras. The introduction with the Venerable Geshe Damcho Yonten was from 8.30 to 9.00, and then lights out was at 10.00. I had a great weekend. It's good to find people who respect life. I thought it was a meditation weekend but instead the session was about karma action with teaching from Geshe Damcho Yonten.

Saturday, 25 November 2000. I was awake at 6.00, and I nearly missed brekkie. A puja was at 6.30, meditation in the lounge was from 7.30 to 8.00, brekkie was from 8.00 to 9.00, and then helping hour, in which I went outside to bag leaves and do other chores, was from 9.00 to 10.00. Then we had teachings from the Ven. Geshe Damcho Yonten from 10.30 to 11.45. After a tea break, we had meditation in the lounge for half an hour starting at 12.45. Lunch followed, and then from 2.00 to 3.00 we had free time. From 3.00 to 4.15 we had more teachings from the Ven. Geshe Damcho Yonten, at 4.25 we had a tea break, and from 4.45 to 5.15 we had meditation. Discussion groups in the lounge lasted from

5.15 to 6.00, and then from 6.00 to 7.00 we had supper, from 7.30 to 8.20 we had the praises and requests to the twenty-one taras, and from 8.30 to 9.30 the Ven. Geshe Damcho Yonten answered questions in the lounge. Lights out was at 1.00.

Sunday, 26 November 2000. Programs started at 6.30, but today I was just about ready for brekkie from 8.00 to 9.00. Helping hour lasted from 9.00 to 10.00, and from 11.45 to 12.15, the Ven. Geshe Damcho Yonten held a teaching session. A tea break followed from 11.45 to 12.15, and at 12.15 was a meditation session. Lunch was from 1.00 to 2.00, and then we said farewell. I was lucky enough to have a lift home off someone from Canton. She is going to give me speech therapy. Emma Lawton, who is partially blind, introduced me to her and arranged a lift. The days at Lam Rim are set out like my diary: they make sure you've always got something to do and somewhere to go.

Monday, 27 November 2000. After an excellent weekend, I ate today, as I stayed down at Lula's and caught up on Wales versus South Africa. Wales lost, but they took South Africa all the way, and the match was very exciting. I then went to Japanese up at Cantonian High from 7.00 to 9.00 and had a taxi home to the flat.

Tuesday, 28 November 2000. I trained in aikido and went for a swim for the first time in more than six weeks. When I was changing, I dithered about and did myself more harm than good. I finally decided that I could be like this for weeks, even months, so I went for it and was fine. My big toe looked healthier afterwards than it had before training.

Wednesday, 29 November 2000. I went to the optician's and ordered yet another new pair of glasses. These are rimless and react to light and cost £320. The last six weeks whilst I've been off swimming and aikido, I've been going to Feldenkrais with Darien Pritchard at the centre. In Feldenkrais, I'm moving parts of the body I didn't know I could move, such as the ribs and ankles. These are very delicate movements, and only someone with a trained eye, such as Peter Gillard, my aikido sensei, and Darien Pritchard, the Feldenkrais practitioner, can see the movements. Everything I do is geared towards improving my mobility. In

Feldenkrais, Pritchard is working on my left shoulder and left arm as well as on my mobility.

Thursday, 30 November 2000. I was up at 9.00-ish and had a taxi to the sports centre for a swim starting at noon. I then walked to the optician's for an eye test. Everything was all right. I then went home to the flat and organized my munchies, chicken and liver and plenty of fruits and vegetables. I then had a lie down for an hour and dozed listening to music. I then ordered a taxi for 7.45 and had a very good aikido session.

Friday, 1 December 2000. I had a taxi to town to see a few people I hadn't seen for about two months. I then went to MNC for CDs and walked down to Lula's. It's *sugoi* (amazing) to see the change in things, especially people. Some are ageing a lot faster than others.

Saturday, 2 December 2000. I had a sporty weekend as usual. I had a taxi down to Lula's, where I watched South Africa versus England in rugby union. I had tea and then walked up to Cardiff Arms Park for Cardiff versus Llanelli. I have a couple of contacts for the book I'm writing. Colin from the bookshop introduced me to a few people. One person who goes to the shop is called Revert. I also phoned the university, so things are looking good at the moment. I walked to Lula's, kipped the night, and had a taxi home the next morning at 9.00. At home I went to bed and rested whilst listening to music. Of course, I was fasting and had to recharge my batteries.

Monday, 4 December 2000. I had a taxi to town. I went to the market to see a few people and then walked down to Lula's for tea and was ready for Japanese from 7.00 to 9.00 at Cantonian High School. I took a taxi there and a taxi back to the flat. I'll stay regular on my aikido and swimming Tuesdays and Thursdays, as I've finally found a good balance of rest and training, although I still occasionally overdo things.

Tuesday, 5 December 2000. I can feel myself improving rapidly after my minor setback with the toe infection. I had a good rest for six weeks from aikido and swimming. The injury was the body's way of telling me to slow down. I walked to the sports centre for a swim and walked back. The toe was fine. At the flat, I got my munchies ready and had a lie down for an hour as I listening to music. I didn't sleep. It does me good to just lie there and rest the body and brain. I then went to aikido from 8.00 to 10.00 at Plasnewydd Community Hall, having a taxi there and back.

Wednesday, 6 December 2000. I went to cash my money and had a Feldenkrais appointment from 2.00 to 3.00. I then had a taxi down to Lula's, where I watched a few aikido tapes and had tea. Then I went home to the flat at about 7.00.

Thursday, 7 December 2000. I fasted yesterday. I cancelled my Feldenkrais till 20 December, as it's my second week back in training. I am going on a Buddhist retreat with John Peacock. I've dithered and changed my mind several times about whether to go on an aikido weekend with Kanetsuka Sensei or on a Buddhist weekend with John Peacock. I think I'll go for a well-deserved rest, as I can feel myself overdoing it again. The rest will do me good. Margaret marked these two retreats off and recommended that I attend. She also gave me a list of recommended courses for next year. I went out at night and watched aikido up at Llanrumney Leisure Centre from 8.30 to 10.00 and picked up a few things. I picked up yet another pair of glasses, which cost £290.70.

Friday, 8 December 2000. I've tried many people who might be proofreaders, one of many ways to get my book off the ground. I went to Headway to get my work from the computer teacher. She was going to do my work, but she didn't have enough time, and it's a lot of work, nearly twelve years all on disk. My mother started keeping diaries of *shigoto* (appointments) we had to attend, and when I was able to, I took them over. It's a *very* slow job. I met Rob in t'ai chi, and he got me a computer and gave me great help getting me started, as I used to do only word processing. I had a taxi to Newport and got there in plenty of time for the 4.10 bus to Raglan for the retreat at Lam Rim Buddhist Centre.

Saturday, 9 December 2000. I changed my mind yet again and decided to go on the aikido course with Kanetsuka Sensei over in Penarth at Arcot Street Church. I couldn't sleep Saturday night and had only about three hours' kip, and then I went to the aikido course from 10.00 to 1.00. It's the first time I've been unable to sleep in years. I must have had things on my mind. The course was a great success, and I picked up a few things. As

I've said, aikido is a very slow martial art. It's not like karate or judo in which you can earn a black belt within two or three years. Aikido involves gradual improvement, which is a great therapy for the brain. I treat aikido like advanced physiotherapy. I went down to Lula's Sunday at about 6.00 as someone phoned about the ad about my autobiography that I placed in Chapter Arts by accident.

Monday, 11 December 2000. I still couldn't sleep. Mother had a *denwa bango* from the proofreader, who is going to phone me tonight to organize a price and other details. I was fasting today, as I had bad guts, and I've found that fasting helps enormously. I went over to Tesco for fruit and up to the health shop. I went to Japanese from Lula's. I filled in the day and tried to catch up with my sleep, but no good.

Tuesday, 12 December 2000. Today was swimming (*oyogo*) at the sports centre and aikido from 8.00 to 10.00 at Plasnewydd Community Hall. I phoned John Bruno, with whom I did Pilates until I had nail surgery for a toe infection. I had the infection for about three years, and it got progressively worse. I don't know how I managed aikido, as I'd be in terrible pain with the infected toe but would just work through the pain.

Tuesday, 12 December 2000. I was completely shattered, but I still went for a swim up at the sports centre. I did my usual lengths except for four, as I was knackered. I walked home in the pouring rain. I was okay with a brolly as it wasn't windy. I gave aikido a rest, as I had a great weekend's training with Kanetsuka Sensei. I contacted Roger, a proofreader, about my book and have to contact him again on 2 January, as he's going away. I was going to suggest that we leave it till after Christmas anyway. Like I've said, before everything has happened at the right time for my improvement. I did a quarter of an hour's meditation in the dark with eyes open last thing at night. It was the first time I've meditated for months, and I went straight off to sleep. I changed my fasting days, and which messed up my body clock.

Wednesday, 13 December 2000. I had a taxi to the ticket line to change trips and went down to Lula's. I ate. Fasting is probably why I haven't been sleeping properly. Like they said up at the hospital, I'd be doing very strange things although they don't seem strange to me. It's all for health and long life.

Thursday, 14 December 2000. I had a taxi to the sports centre for a swim and walked back. I went to aikido at 8.30. The last two weeks I've done sit-ups with the aerobics class starting at 8.10 before aikido at 8.30. This week in aikido we had a blackout when we were warming up, so we trained for about five minutes and had to evacuate the building in the pitch black. I later found out the whole of Llanrumney was blacked out for three-quarters of an hour. I was lucky enough to have a lift to town. I stayed the night at Lula's.

Friday, 15 December 2000. I had a taxi to Headway to pick up my disks from Maureen, who was going to do my book but finally gave it up as she didn't have the time. I've been putting up ads about it, and I've got a professional proofreader called Roger who is going to do the work for me. I have to contact him in the new year. It'll be a great start to the year. I then travelled down to Lula's and watched a few videos on sightings, as I was not eating, and I walked home to the flat at about 6.00. I bought a plot of land on the moon from Waterstones. I have to register it. It seems a bit far-fetched, but I've been watching a lot of space programmes on the Discovery Channel. When you think of it, it's amazing the progress we've made in one hundred years, so anything's possible.

Saturday, 16 December 2000. I fasted today, as tomorrow is the last day I'll be able to till 8 January, so I'll have a good swim tomorrow and have a bet on the horses in the afternoon. I watched the rugby at 5.30 and boxing at 8.00. Boxing had four world-title fights, including one with Welshman Joe Kalzage versus Woodhall.

Sunday, 17 December 2000. I watched Man United versus Liverpool at 11.00. I was then going to go swimming at the sports centre, but my sister called and took me over to the bay for a new video, which will be my Christmas present to myself. Emma Langton phoned to say she had a lift to Lam Rim Buddhist Centre on Tuesday, so it will save me going by taxi and bus, but she's not going home to Cardiff, so I will play it by ear for a lift home. If I can't get a lift, I'll go on the buss, changing at Newport as I've done before. I'll go up to my sister's on Tuesday, as she lives around the corner from Tesco. I have to be at Emma's at 5.00 for the lift off Simon.

Monday, 18 December 2000. I had a taxi to town and went to the market and other shops, and then I walked down to Lula's, had tea, and watched a few science videos. Then I had a taxi home at 6.30 and got my bag ready for Lam Rim, where I'm going Tuesday night at 5.00. I went up to my sister Julie's and had tea before going off to Emma's at 5.00. Emma lives about a five-minute drive from Julie. We arrived at Lam Rim at around 6.00 and then we had soup and did a puja. I've done that before, but that was on a special day at a kum nye course with John Peacock. This was the fourth time I've stayed at Lam Rim. I'm becoming a Buddhist very slowly. It started off with chi kung with Len Sinclair. A few of the boys at chi kung were going to a Buddhist talk up in Bristol for the day, so I tagged along. I continued going on day courses and day trips to Lam Rim with Len Sinclair in the last few years stayed at Lam Rim three times. It is very peaceful there and the people are decent. They don't drink or smoke, or so they say. When I was a Jehovah's Witness, people weren't supposed to smoke or drink, but most of them did occasionally. Wednesday the 20th is the anniversary of Lama Tsong Khapa, and I'll spend the day with the Ven. Geshe Damcho Yonten and return on Thursday. After puja Tuesday, night I was lost, so I asked for a lift to the bus stop, but the course attendee who drove me very generously gave me a lift all the way to Lula's. I gave him a tenner for the trouble. When I arrived at Lula's, my sister and auntie laughed their heads off. If I decide not to stay somewhere, I just up and go. That happened when I was in Spain with two other Jehovah's Witnesses. I up and flew home and caught a train from Piccadilly.

When I was on crutches, I used to time myself on walks starting off at Lula's. I would meet quit a lot of people who gave me great encouragement, mostly older people. There were Stella and Jack in Penarth Road (Stella has since passed on), Reg and Mrs Ralph, whom I knew from junior school, and many others who stopped to have a chat with me and give me great encouragement.

Thursday, 21 December 2000. I fasted today, although I had a bit of fruit. I walked down to the post office to cash my money and then went over to Chapter Arts to study Japanese (*yubikyokyo*) and reading my books (*hons*). I do this a few times a week. You'd be surprised how much Japanese I learn. I read the material over and over again and things register. We are on to verbs, pronouns, and adjectives, and it is very difficult. It's much harder for me than for other students, as I'm slower, but I remember with repetition. In the new year, Emma (a Buddhist) is go to invite her Japanese artist friend and me for private tuition. I'll have to take the books which I study from to her so she can see what stage I'm at. Japanese is a very difficult subject. It's a lifelong process like aikido.

Friday, 22 December 2000. I walked to town as I had no training or courses. I walked to the flats in Cowbridge Road at the bottom of Cathedral Road. I went in out of curiosity and was talking to the doorman. The flats seem a good buy. From there, I walked to the market and saw Colin from the bookshop. He said that Darlows have gone into liquidation, so I walked back down to the flats and into the Darlows office. I found out that it has just changed ownership, so I've arranged to visit the property and to have my flat valued. The janitor said there would be old couples around me, so it's nice and quiet. I arrived home and had tea and a bath at about 5.00 and went over to Chapter Arts at 6.15 for *Small Time Crooks*, a Woody Allen film. I decided to go down to Lula's for Christmas after I arrived home at 8.00. I had a taxi down and stayed the night and came back home at noon on Saturday. I did not like the noise from next door, of people coming in and out of Lula's, and the smoking. You can't expect people to not smoke because of me, and I've got weird quirks since the accident, so I'm better off in my own flat on my own.

Sunday, 24 December 2000. I fasted today and was happy to be back in my own environment. I did my usual stuff, watching videos of aikido and sports and, of course, going on my computer, just filling in my day. There was plenty to watch on TV, as I've got cable, especially on Discovery.

Saturday, 23 December 2000. I went down to the rugby union to see Cardiff versus Pontypridd, walking their and back. Afterwards, I had my tea, chicken and veg, and settled down for the boxing and footie at 10.30.

Sunday, 24 December 2000. I fasted today and carried on with my fifteen-minute meditation last thing. It's Crimbo Eve, and I'm quite happy to be on my own, as I have strange ideas mainly to do with health.

Monday, 25 December 2000. Crimbo Day. I've been waking at 9.40 the last four days. I had brekkie and listened to music as usual and went for a walk from 1.15 to 2.15. When I got in, I had a bath in time for my sightings programme on the Discovery Channel and then made my Crimbo dinner: liver, beans, fresh tomatoes, and raw veg. Then I settled down for an evening's viewing.

Tuesday, 26 December 2000. Boxing Day. I had a bet and walked down to Lula's. I watched racing from 12.30 to 3.00 and straight after was Cardiff versus Newport in rugby union. I had tea at 5.00 and walked home at about 7.00. It took half an hour, but I don't mind walking, as I'm on my holidays. When I'm back to aikido and swimming, I'll have taxis instead, as walking gets you tired before you start, which I did before. I have learned by my mistakes all along.

Wednesday, 27 December 2000. I was fasting today, and I walked down to Lula's. I had a bet on the way down and cancelled my appointment to view flats, as I don't think I'll get a better place than where I am at the moment, with Tesco over the road and Chapter Arts, the post office, the Principality, and the library nearby, the location is pretty central. I had an afternoon's viewing when I had a bet and had a taxi back at about 7.00, as I had to carry presents and other items.

Thursday, 28 December 2000. Bolke Raith was coming between 7.00 and 9.00 tonight, so I walked down Lula's and spent the afternoon there watching a tape of programmes from the Discovery Channel that I had made earlier. I was waiting for Raith to come so I could train in aikido up at Llanrumney Leisure Centre. I did twenty minutes of stretching and sit-ups, so I had the buzz although I was going to rest till the new year.

Friday, 29 December 2000. Still snow and ice on the roads. I again walked down to Lula's to visit and passing the time. Just New Year's Eve to go now. I must admit, I don't like Crimbo, so I'm just passing the time. I'm still happy as Larry, and I think I'm

133

going to have a good future. Well, I don't think, I know. I have to phone Roger the proofreader on 2 January. I think we'll all be living in space in the future. I've bought eleven acres on the moon, one acre from Waterstones for £20 and the other ten acres from Moon Products.

Saturday, 30 December 2000. It has been snowing the last few days, and it's changed to ice now, making the roads very dangerous. It's okay if you stick to main roads. I walked down to Lula's, taking it very slowly, and had a bet on the way down. I was in the betting office five minutes before the first race at Lingfield, the all-weather track, as all the other meetings were abandoned. I put my bet on 1 in the early race and on 3 on the telly. They showed a recording of the first race purely out of interest to fill in the time. It was supposed to start at 1.45 but was called off just before racing started, so I'll keep my ticket and have a bet of only a fiver on New Year's Day. I bought a skipping rope a few months ago to improve my balance and co-ordination, and Steven, Julie's boyfriend, showed me how to use it. At the beginning, I couldn't even jump, but time is a great healer, and I continue to improve. Raith the video man was coming at 7.00, so I got back to get ready for him.

Sunday, 31 December 2000. New Year's Eve. I was fasting. I went to the bin, but it had all iced over, so I took the rubbish back in and went to Tesco for paper, holding on to railings on the way, as it was very icy, and then walked on the road. On the way back, I couldn't get back in, so someone came and helped me. I was lucky that I had a boxing tape with me to watch down at Lula's. I remember a programme I watched on the mind that said that people who have a bang to the left side of the temporal lobe have psychic abilities. I used to have dreams about horses, and they'd come in at good prices. I also had a dream that I'd live till I was 161. I saw a really good programme about the space station. That's where the future lies. That lunar land I bought is looking good, but it won't be liveable in a couple of years; it'll be more like fifty years, but I'm going to live for 161 years, so there's no rush. Everything is starting to fit in and make sense for a very long life. I think I'll spend it on the moon. When I tell people this, everyone just laughs, but I'll have the last laugh.

Monday, 1 January 2001. I walked down to Lula's, had a bet, and stayed down there till about 6.00. Then I walked home to the flat.

Tuesday, 2 January 2001. I have to phone Roger the proofreader to talk about what I want to do and to arrange the money. He reckons I could get funding off the government if I give them a small piece of my work.

Wednesday, 3 January 2001. I went to Feldenkrais with Darien Pritchard at the centre. I've been to aikido twice this week, Tuesday and Thursday, and Feldenkrais and aikido go together. In aikido the aim is to become soft and supple, and Feldenkrais has the same goal. I was lucky enough to read about Feldenkrais in an aikido magazine after about a year's training in aikido and was lucky enough to find a practitioner in Cardiff, Darien Pritchard. I started with him once a month and then started going for a treatment every week for the six weeks I was inactive because of my toe. I've started this year off with the goal of training in aikido twice a week, Tuesday and Thursday, and swimming on and Feldenkrais on Wednesday. I'll fill up the rest of the time with Japanese. Everything is pointing to me moving to Japan. I spent the last few years trying out different healing techniques. This year I'm going to try one more healing technique, dowsing, with Jack Temple. He holds workshops over at Chapter Arts, so it's well handy. I'm really only going to meet girls, as there were a lot of females at his talk at the students' union. I believe everybody has healing abilities but only some people channel theirs correctly. I phoned up Roger the proofreader, and he's coming tonight for a chat. As I have said earlier, I always knew I'd have this accident, do everything I'm doing at the moment, and live a very long, healthy life by eating plenty of fruits and vegetables, not smoking, and not drinking the demon's brew. I see myself living till I'm 161.

Chapter 8

January 2001. I contacted a proofreader with a view to writing a book in the very early stages. I continued with my aikido twice week, swimming twice a week, Feldenkrais with Darien Pritchard, and Japanese lessons. At this stage, I was fasting on Sundays and occasionally on Wednesdays also. I was also going to aikido courses with Kanetsuka Sensei.

I also went to Lam Rim Buddhist Centre for a kum nye course with John Peacock on 6, 7, and 8 April 2001 and for an Easter retreat. I moved flats to Bakers Court on 26 April. I went to the Natural Health Show 28 and 29 April and had been fasting for seven years, eleven months, and one week. I had another retreat, a mindfulness retreat, at Raglan Buddhist Centre.

I was also going for Zero Balancing treatments. I did aikido courses at Aberdare, Port Talbot, and Penarth. I did another kum nye retreat with John Peacock at Lam Rim Buddhist centre in Raglan. I also went to Jehovah's Witness meetings on Sundays, as a staff nurse who lived opposite my mother roped me into going to meetings, but they don't make a lot of sense. I had another aikido course at Aberdare. I was having Japanese lessons from Naoko Sugayama, and I gave her structured English lessons. I had done a TEFL course, which is an English course to teach the language to foreigners. I went to aikido summer camp at Chester on 4 August. I was doing t'ai chi at Severn Road and did a few more aikido courses. I did a mind and body course and a mind, brain, and science course at Cardiff University.

January 2002. I went to see Dr Lam, who is a chi kung master at Riverside, for a short time. I continued with my aikido and swimming whilst also taking a t'ai chi class at Grass Roots and Japanese with Naoko Sugayama. I continued teaching her English and attending a TEFL course on Monday nights and a mind, brain, and science course.

I went on holiday to Turkey at the end of May 2002. I was also learning Japanese at Severn Road with Jane Kajemoto and training in NIA, a sort of dancing yoga. At the end of November, I saw an advert for Thai introductions, so as my life was going nowhere, I phoned up and booked a flight over to Thailand in January 2003. I met my wife, Lalita, at the office. It usually takes two or three dates to know if you're a match, but Lalita and I hit it off straight away. I went back and got married in April 2003 but continued flying back and forth until she got her visa. I stayed in Thailand for seven months, including over Christmas 2004. Brian Snelgrove up at the students' union told me that I'd become a healer but that it wouldn't happen overnight; it would be a very, very slow job. We went to Lalita's new home, and then in the summer of 2005, we went to Brecon Jazz Festival. Lalita liked Brecon, so we ended up buying a house there. I went back and forth to Cardiff to have driving lessons in an automatic car, as there were no automatic driving instructors at Brecon. We ended up buying an automatic car, and our friend Colin Jones used to take me out a few times a week. I sat four tests up in Brecon, all with Colin Jones as my driving instructor. We flew back and forth to Thailand at the time too.

2007. I was having driving lessons with BSM. I went from Brecon to Cwmbran to do a gym instructors' course on 11 and 12 February. I passed the time up at Brecon by going to the gym and swimming and going to aikido with the British Aikido Board. I went to a British Aikido Federation course at Swansea with Kanetsuka Sensei on 17 February.

I had another weekend away for the gym instructors' course. I did another theory paper as my two years were nearly up. I was now with Red Dragon Driving School in Cardiff, learning in an automatic, of course. Colin Jones still instructed me, and I could feel myself improving rapidly. I was getting my balance on the road and not veering as much as I had except when I got tired. It's amazing how the brain regenerates itself, repairing injured parts.

23 April 2007. I tried an intensive driving course, and after three days the instructor gave me a refund and said with my brain injury, it's going to be a very slow job. I already knew that, but I just thought I'd try.

Bob at Red Dragon took me for another driving assessment on the request of Pat McKenna, the head neurologist at Rookward.

Pat McKenna phoned Bob and told him I shouldn't be driving, but Bob said if I wanted to drive, he'd get me through my test.

30 May 2007. I had another driving lesson in an automatic.

Every Sunday I went for a swim then get changed for aikido.

I continued with my driving, aikido, and swimming. I continued with driving lessons and went to and fro with Bob. I was booking ten lessons at a time. I was also into complementary therapies and continued with t'ai chi, practicing in the house if I had no class. I was back with BSM in July. I joined the centre down at the sports village, as they offered t'ai chi and swimming. I also got another driving instructor.

January 2011. I continued with my aikido and swimming twice a week and did t'ai chi on Sundays. I went to Severn Road to see what form of t'ai chi they were doing, and I met the instructor. By chance, he turned out to be the master who had taught the person I had trained with for a year at the sports village. When Brian Snelgrove at the students' union told me I'd become a healer, I hadn't realised it yet, but aikido and t'ai chi are the therapies I'll use.

The first six months or more I went to t'ai chi three times a week with the same instructor. I also sat a few more driving tests in Cardiff.

I booked another ten driving lessons with Uncle Bob, as I call him, at Red Dragon Driving School and alternated those with lessons from BSM. I continued with my t'ai chi twice on Tuesday and on Thursday. I enrolled in a t'ai chi seminar for 1 October. I had a test in November with Uncle Bob, and I had my thirteenth driving test on 6 January 2012. I passed after twelve years of trying and being told not to drive.

A letter from Bob.

My name is Bob Wall. I am a driving instructor with Red Dragon Driving School based in Cardiff.

I have been an instructor for nearly twenty years, the last twelve helping people with disabilities. It is work that gives me a lot of satisfaction.

A few years ago, I met Andrew Penman, who travelled from Brecon to Cardiff to be helped with his driving with a view to passing his driving test. He told me he had sat several tests, a couple in Cardiff and four in Brecon, to no avail.

On talking to Andrew, he told me that he had received brain damage.

On the road, Andrew's road positioning was terrible. He drove close to parked cars, and he did not look far ahead to see situations; he just drove straight into them. I knew my work was cut out for me from the off.

Several times Andrew asked me about a driving test, but I told him he was not ready, so off he went, I think four times, with other instructors. I think he sat four tests in Brecon and six in Cardiff.

But after each one, he still came back to me.

Then one day he finally started to listen to me, and the improvement was like a fairy tale. I gave the go-ahead for a test, and he passed on his second time with me. Hooray! But no, that's not the end. He wants me to take him to Rookward Hospital so he can tell them, 'Look, people with brain damage can still drive.' He told me he was not interested in buying a car; he just wanted to prove a point.

Well, I blew my top with all the work I have done, and he did it just to prove a point.

If you put this in your book, Andrew, know that you are not the first person I have taught with brain damage, but you are the most stubborn, and the way you just came bouncing back to me, I had to admire you. Best of luck now, and get yourself a car and take your wife and your dogs a bit further than Grangetown.

All the best,
Bob